ISBN-978-1460968284

Dragos Roua

Assess Decide Do

Natural Productivity

The bricks and mortar for building your own life management framework. A practical guide for using a real life application for time, task and projects management. For lifestyle DIY junkies only.

Table Of Contents

4

Foreword

This ebook is based on one of my content products launched a year ago. For those of you who had a chance to get "30 Sentences For A Millionaire Mindset" the first part of this ebook, especially, will seem extremely familiar. In the initial package for 30 Sentences, the Assess - Decide - Do was just a booklet.

Over the last year, the ideas in my framework grew up steady and the booklet become bigger than just a few pages. It become a full product, with much more content, with an improved workflow and with a companion iPhone / iPad app. I use this life management framework daily (more on what is a life management framework in the Introduction) and I also expanded it in other areas, trying to prove its efficiency.

A few months before publishing the first edition of this book I launched iAdd, the iPhone/iPad productivity app based on Assess - Decide - Do. I coded the app myself, applying many techniques described in my own framework. At some point, even the development process of the app was managed by the app itself. I actually used it to build it. All the planning, debugging and testing was made by assessing, deciding and doing using iAdd.

An important part of this ebook will contain a guide on how to use iAdd for iPhone/iPad. So, rest assured that what you're going to read will not be just fluffy, abstract or esoteric blah-blah. It's down to earth, day to day life, explained and improved. But for some of you that like blah-blah, I still kept some. ;-)

HOW TO READ THIS BOOK

The short answer: from top to bottom. The long answer: there are 3 main logical levels of this ebook, organized pretty much in the same way: from top, ethereal ideas, to the grounded, day to day activities.

The first level is the most philosophical one. Don't get the term "philosophical" in its "incredibly hard to grasp" sense, but rather in its "theoretical" or "from the bird view" sense. It will be a part where you could follow the ideas behind the framework and even speculating about them. You'll understand the concepts, you're going to play with them in various contexts and you may even challenge them if you feel the need. It's the part where you could start and stop reading at your ease. It's the introductory part.

The second level is about potential practical uses of the framework. There are a few real life examples of using "Assess - Decide - Do" in various scenarios, from relationships, natural productivity or personal crisis management. It's the practical part.

And the third level is the most "tutorialized" one. It will contain a very detailed and practical description of iAdd for iPhone / iPad and a few of the recommended uses. That is the "DIY" part of the book. Once you will understand the ins and outs of the iPhone / iPad app (which is really simple and intuitive, by the way, if I'd have to believe all the reviews on the AppStore ;-)), you will have a real tool based on Assess - Decide - Do to work with day in and day out.

As you can see, the book follows the main "Assess - Decide - Do" paradigm in itself. You get a chance to assess the idea, decide in which part of your life you are going to apply them and then actually do them using a real life tool.

***

At the end of this short foreword, I want to send a big "Thank You" to all my blog readers, fellow bloggers and social media followers. No idea can grow by itself, it needs good soil, light and support. And I got a lot of light and support from hundreds of thousands of people in the last 2 years, since I started dragosroua.com. I feel enriched by them and I'm grateful for their support.

Thank You :-)

Introduction

Life management is one of those things we're not quite aware of until we observe, one way or another, that our own life is a mess. Life management is a neutral name for a large collection of habits, strategies, rules, religions, philosophies and patterns on which we are relying every day in living our lives. Life management is one of those things that affects us even if we're not aware of their existence.

I started to consciously manage my life several years ago, after 3 decades of drifting away from one pattern to another, from one job to another, from one relationship to another. It was a conscious choice which led me to a beautiful journey. It wasn't something deeply enlightening or brutally disruptive, but rather a slow process of awakening in which I started to put together informations, to create habits, to initiate relationships and to create things around me. It actually took me several years to even understand that I started something called life management.

And that happened when I realized that I can actually recreate my apparently random moments of happiness and fulfillment almost whenever I want to. When I realized that I can interpret and modify reality in a way which would be completely personal and totally rewarding at the same time. When I realized that I am the creator of my own circumstances, not the victim of those so-called bad timings.

Life management is the process of consciously living your life. You can be good at this, or you can be bad. I'm not talking here about success in terms of cultural definitions (which can include money, a certain lifestyle or access to power). The way you live your life is entirely your choice. You can choose to acquire wealth or you can chose to acquire only respect.

Whatever you choose is your life goal. Life management is how you stick to this goal.

As any management process, this can be improved. You can make it better. Or you can make it worse, of course. As a matter of fact, even if you think you're not managing your life right now, in fact, you're doing it. And you're doing it pretty bad, of course, letting it slipping through your fingers.

This book will describe a framework for life management. A framework that proved to do a good job for my own life. And being just a framework, it's not a rigid system, but merely a scaffold. It's not in a fixed structure but rather in light, flexible concepts. It's not even finished as it is intended to be finished by you, with your own experience. It's something that you can build upon.

A framework for your own life management system.

Part One: What Is ADD?

A Life Management System

ADD is a framework for life management. It comes from the abbreviation of its 3 main elements or states:

Assess - Decide - Do

Any activity in your life, from the tiniest habitual task to the most complex long term project you undertake can be broke down in these 3 states. At any moment in your life your focus is centered in one of those states.

Most of our failures in life management are forms of a focus imbalance. We either can't calibrate enough of our focus in one of those states, affecting their quality, their power, or we mix those states, affecting their purity, their efficiency. Any problem we face is in fact a weak link in our assess-decide-do flow.

A successful life management is just a constant flow in and out of these states in the aforementioned order, while maintaining a higher degree of purity for each of them. A constant and steady focus on each of these states, followed by a smooth flow to the next state is the key for successful life management.

THE ASSESS STATE

This is the reflective state of your being. It's a state in which you are collecting data from your internal reality as well as from your external circumstances. It's a state in which you are evaluating where you are in terms of alignment with your desired outcome.

As such, you can assess your current situation, your options, your goals, the progress you've made so far, unexpected modifications, new outcomes, etc. Assessment is an analytic state.

The assessment process doesn't have a fixed duration, it's a function of your current situation and your previous experience. Each assessment is considered complete when you have a clear conclusion that explains and validates the assessment process. More on that on the chapter dedicated to this state.

THE DECIDE STATE

This is the projective state of your being. In this state you are making projections of what you want to do next. You create your next milestone by using metaphors: words, images, shapes.

As such, you can decide to follow a certain path, to create a certain object, to engage in a certain relationship or to cease some activity, to abandon a project, etc. Decision is an active state.

The decision process also doesn't have a fixed duration, it's a function of the assessment process and your previous experience. Each decision state is considered finished when you have a clear and definable outcome that validates the assessment and invalidates the decision process to the level it's not necessary anymore.

In other words, a decision stage is consumed when you know exactly what you have to do. More on that on the chapter dedicated to this state.

THE DO STATE

This is the creative state of your being. In this state you are actually doing what you decided to do after you assessed your current situation. This is where you actually create your reality.

In this state you are totally immersed in your own world, your actions are directly influencing your reality and you are experiencing a very close interaction with your environment. Your "do" state is a flow state.

The do process will last as long as needed in order to validate the decision process. The moment you reached the goal you've set on the "decision" state you move to a new assessment state again. Most of our time is spent on the "do" state as it is the most rewarding one in terms of sensorial experience. Almost any kind of joy and fulfillment in our life comes from the "do" state.

Do leads to Assess whenever you step out from the present, whenever your focus is weakened and needs reinforcement.

***

Assess: your current situation, your options, your goals

Decide: establish if you're doing or not what you assessed, chose an option, chose a path

Do: walk your path, enjoy it, be there, be in the moment, in the present, in the now and here

The 5 Elements Of ADD

ADD is made of 5 elements: the 3 stages or realms, defined above and 2 components that brings everything together: focus and flow.

Very briefly, focus is what puts you in each realm and the tool by which you experience that realm, while flow is a state of congruence both in performing in that realm and in switching from one realm to another.

Now lets' get into details.

ASSESS

You don't have to do everything on your agenda, you know? Well, unless you're a robot with no self-awareness and free will.

You do have the freedom to assess everything around and take into account as much information as you can about any specific task.

Assessing is one of the most ignored states of the contemporary, modern individual. When you run furiously in your own rat race trap, you really don't have time to assess, you just run.

I find assessing vital for a successful outcome of any task, goal or activity I start. If I'm not assessing it enough, if I'm not integrating it into my own personal system of values, bad things are happening. I mean, I might get that thing done, but I won't be so happy about it. To say the least. Doing something against your personal values is one of the worst things you can do to yourself.

Integrating a specific task in your personal system of values is, of course, only one of the things you may want to do in the assessment stage. You can have tons of other things to assess, like the short or long term benefits, the opportunity, the resources availability and so on. All of this must be done in the Assess realm.

I realize that assessing has a cumulative structure. I put together pieces of information, emotions, memories, until I come up with a specific object. When I can't add to it anymore, when it looks the same to me regardless of my standpoint, I know it's time to make a decision. Then, and only then, I can move to the decision realm.

Let's see some of the most typical activities you perform in the Assess realm.

Evaluation

The Assess realm is the place where you will do all of your evaluation. You can evaluate your current situation, the outcome of a previously completed task, a possible outcome for a possible task; in one word: everything. In the evaluation process you don't necessarily have to DO, or DECIDE anything. The moment you put some pressure for DECIDING or DOING on the assessment, you affect its purity.

Evaluating without the pressure of a decision or a deadline is a very necessary step. Too often I found myself lost in a decisional process or even in the middle of a larger project because I skipped or under-considered the evaluation/assessment step. Assessing something means you're simply looking at something, you're acknowledging the fact that something new (or worthwhile) have entered your focus.

Evaluation is only one of the possible activities in an assessment stage, but it's usually the one that ends this very stage, by promoting the idea, the project or the task to the decision realm.

Information Management

The assessment stage is the one in which you'll do most of your information management. Crunching new pieces of information, categorizing them, putting them higher or lower in your value system is an activity which takes place in the assessment stage. Again, mixing it with a decision or a doing realm will do no good, as it will either slow down the decision or the doing process, or contaminate it with undesired pieces of information.

Managing information is a static activity in itself. You're not doing anything – doing, as in modifying your universe – while you're managing information, you're just classifying various inputs from the outside (or the inside world).

Getting Feedback

As the name implies, feedback is an activity which takes place immediately after something was done, after something has been modified in your own universe. Assessing feedback is a crucial activity in the assessment stage, it really helps you understand if your actions were improving (or not) your environment.

You take feedback by comparing your initial status, the moment you started modifying something in your universe, with your current status. You will receive feedback from a wide variety of sources: your physical senses (as in it's colder or warmer than before), your emotions (this thing makes me feel in a certain way), your memories (this looks a lot like something I've done before) or the people you interact with.

Feedback is usually one of the earliest activities in the assessment stage, as it is often immediately required after an action has been finished.

Observation

Assessment cannot work without fresh information, without being constantly fed with new data. It needs this as a comparison outlet. In the assessment stage you'll observe a lot. Observation is an activity closely related to information management, but its place is at the very beginning of the information management chain. Observation is the input for the information management activity.

As any input, the clearer and less distorted, the best the results. Observing things as they are, and not as you imagine they are is an art in itself. Training observation is a difficult and delicate activity. Becoming a detached observer will make your assessment periods shorter.

Dreaming

Dreaming is the capacity of imagining things which are not yet real. Dreaming plays a very big part in the assessment period. Most of the time, you decide to do things based on deep and extremely emotional inputs, coming from what you call your dreams. Creating a newer and better reality comes from dreaming first, from the ability to imagine unborn things and ignite the triggers to create them.

The classical approach to dreaming is to either discard it totally as completely unproductive, or to classify it as procrastination, the activity in which you are preventing yourself from doing things, by inventing excuses. I do think dreaming is fundamental and is a very productive activity. As long as you acknowledge it as a very necessary step in the assessment realm.

Memories

The things you're doing are becoming memories the moment you finish them. Accessing your memories is an important part of your life. It helps maintain an identity and a sense of coherence in time. Without memories, your perspective can become twisted. Most of the time, your value system is based on things you recall as being good or bad to you.

Keeping your memories in good shape – like in creating and maintaining a memories management system – will hugely impact your overall presence. Only after you understand the past you, can the present you can become a reality. One very common pitfall in the assessment stage is clogging your perspective with unsolved memories, with things from the past which are crying for a newer approach.

Solving those situations in the assessment stage will take a lot of pressure from your decision and doing realms.

Meditation

Assessment needs a clear perspective. When you decide, you start to move, when you do, you are the movement, but when you assess, your whole world can slow down, until it becomes stillness. Nobody will rush you. Meditation is one precious activity which can dramatically enhance your perspective. Seeing the world from a still perspective is enlightening. Meditation can do that.

Of course, is not compulsory to use all of the activities described here, including meditation. As a matter of fact, in real life, it would be rather difficult to identify all those activities in an assessment session at the same time.

When To Move To Decision

The moment you stop assessing something you should immediately move to the decision realm. Staying in the assessment realm for longer periods can induce a sense of comfort and security, which, if not rapidly challenged, will be modified pretty soon by "outside" factors. In other words, if you don't move faster, something outside your control will force you to do it.

One thing we should definitely want to remember about assessment, and about the whole ADD paradigm, is that any process can contain smaller, or micro-ADD cycles. During the assessment cycle you may find the need to quickly decide and then do something, and then come back to your main assessment topic. In this respect, ADD is very close to the fractals definitions, in which the smaller parts are actually identical with the bigger parts.

But more on that in the next topic, which will be, of course, about the decision realm.

DECIDE

As opposed to assessing, decision is a one point structure. Once you can't assess anything anymore, you decide what to do about it. You have only 2 options:

- Do it
- Don't do it

If you decide to do it, you'll move to the Doing realm. If you decide not to do it, you'll discard the task completely. The nice thing about this dual attitude is that you won't have to postpone it. You simply decide you won't do it, period. You have the freedom to discard it completely or to move it back to the Assessment realm. If you can't do it now, maybe the future will bring some more info and you'll be in a better position to make a decision. But you made a decision about it, you can move on.

If I know I have to make a decision about a specific topic I usually do it within a very small time span.

Several minutes up to maximum 24 hours. I'm talking about regular, normal tasks like blogging or business. There are some situations in which the decision part can last several months, like moving to a new country or relationship decisions. But if there's something within my current time horizon, I don't delay it more than 24 hours.

Being in the Assessment realm before has a very big advantage: I already have all the info I need to work with. Now, if I decided I'll go further, all I have to do is to move into the Doing realm.

The Decide realm is the place in which you intend to change your reality. You get in, put up the intention to modify your reality, and then you get out of it. You move immediately in the Do realm. The Decide realm nature is disruptive and powerful. It really challenges your current reality and it does this with a lot of force. It's a hit and run approach. And it's supposed to be like this.

As opposed to the Assess realm, where you can spend hours, days, weeks or months, the Decide realm is a very short sighted one. You don't live long in the Decide realm. If you do, you have an ADD imbalance (more on life imbalances explained with ADD in a separate chapter). That decision-delay-imbalance would be the so-called someday syndrome, a situation in which you allegedly know what you have to do, but never really commit to it. You remain stuck in this decision realm for ever.

Decision Is On The Inside

How do you know you actually took a decision and you're not still in the Assess realm? How do you know it's time to make a decision in the first place? How do you make that decision?

For many of us, decision seems to be driven by outside factors. We have to go to the job, we have to move out of the house for errands, we have to pay our mortgage. We make these decisions in response to outside factors. Once we took the decision, we start moving. Go to the job, to the grocery shop, we pay the bills.

In fact, the decision is never driven by outside factors, it's an internal process.

We make a decision after we can no longer assess the facts. If there's nothing more to assess about our mortgage payment we make a decision: pay it. Or don't pay it, of course. If we can't assess anything more about the job, we go there, we immerse in the task. If it's nothing more to add about our grocery shopping list, we go shopping. Or don't and give room to other events in our life.

Decision Is A Reality Killer

Each decision you take will kill your current reality and will force you to replace it with another one, by going into the Do realm. You can recognize a decision by its level of reality destruction. If the decision will not change something in your reality, it's not a decision, it's still an assessment. If the decision will dramatically change your reality, you know it's time to move on and create that reality.

For example, if you decide to go to your job, that will dramatically change your current environment: you'll be in a different room, talking with different people and doing something different from what you're doing now. If you're going to the grocery shop, you'll alter your reality by bringing in some more items. If you pay your mortgage, your reality will be modified also: you'll have less money and you'll be closer to completely pay off your house.

So, the simplest and most accurate sign for recognizing a decision is its capacity of changing reality. If it's not projecting a new reality, different from your current one, you're not actually making a decision, you're playing with your mind.

Choosing Your Personal Path

Taking the right decision is an art, so it's living in the Assess realm, and it's doing things in the Do realm. Identifying the best decision you can take at a certain point in your life is a key factor in your life management framework. In fact, your personal growth and evolution are dictated by your decisions, not by your assessment, nor by doing. It's what you decide that creates your reality, doing it is just an effect, not a cause.

You're taking at least one decision each minute. You drive your focus and create your next reality all the time. Sadly, most of the time you're doing it on auto-pilot. Without assessing. You're just following old habits or established patterns. You're living by reflex, not by miracle. Each decision you take is really a small miracle, because it reveals your creative powers. With each decision you actually modify your universe and create your desired world.

The core of your existence is in the Decision realm. The power of your self transformation is there, in the decision you take, in the realities you project for yourself, in the future you already see and embrace. So, instead of going to a job, assess more and see if that job really fits you. Instead of going to the grocery shop see if you can do something more interesting with your time. Instead of paying your mortgage see if you can pay it all in one leap.

Maybe the answer to all these will be: ok, I've assessed it and I can't do anything about it right now. I'll go to that job, I'll go shopping and then I'll pay my bill. But if you do this assessment constantly, something will change. Your decision will be influenced. Maybe after a while you'll understand that your job is not fulfilling, is something you'd like to change, and with this everything will change.

What you've just done is to break an old, petrified flow in the Assess-Decide-Do pattern and create a new one. This is how life changes.

Small Decisions Or Big Decisions?

The power of a life management framework resides in its flexibility, in its power to adapt and adjust. You can apply this pattern to all processes, from your lifetime destiny and fulfillment to your day to day activities. As long as you correctly identify each stage in which you are acting, you have the power to rewrite those patterns.

There are no small or big decisions. Each decision is important and each decision has the power to change your world.

Do

Here is the place for mainstream methodologies like GTD. Here is the place in which I look over my lists, do the associated tasks and actually check them as done. If there's something on my Do list, I know I already passed through 2 filters: Assess and Decide, so I don't have anything left to do about that task. Except doing it, of course.

The Do realm can be repetitive and can last days or months. It's not a cumulative structure, although it can produce visible results, and it's not a one point structure. It's more like a flow. It's not unusual to be in the Doing stage for months, if I have a larger project, coding, for instance.

Whenever I finish doing some task or project, I go back to the Assessment realm, closing the circle. At this point, I finished an ADD cycle in which I included a lot of activities, from assessment, to decision making and to actually doing the specific project.

Usually, whenever I finish an ADD cycle I have a very deep and powerful sense of well being. Every cycle I finish adds to my self-respect in a way I never experienced before. Every ADD cycle is very different than a checked task on a list, it's more like reaching the next level on a spiral path.

The Physical World

The Do realm is where you are closing the circle you started to draw by assessing and then deciding something. It's the final stage and the most physical one. Usually, what you're doing is something touchable, real, as opposed to the Assess or Decide stages, which are mainly mental activities. The Do realm is like the visible part of an iceberg. You know an iceberg can show only a small part on the surface, and this is the Do realm, but the core of it is under the water, in the initial Assess and Decide stages.

The Do realm is also one of the most refined and talked about by productivity experts. Much of the writing and methodologies created in the productivity area are focusing only on the Do realm, including GTD. Productivity and effectiveness are mistakenly defined as a consequence of the Do realm, when in fact they are a consequence of an entire Assess – Decide – Do cycle.

If you did your job in the Assess and Decide stages, you're not actually doing much in the Do realm. There are only 3 main related activities on the Do realm, and these are scheduling, prioritizing and finishing.

Scheduling

Don't think of scheduling in terms of assigning a certain time frame to a task, this is done in the Decide. Scheduling in the Do realm means more of a way to postpone what you don't want or have to do now. Even in the Do realm, you have limited resources. So you have to focus on what you can be done in the current context. As such, you may (and, to be honest, you will) reschedule a lot of activities, based on your current availability.

As any other activity, scheduling can be improved, refined and automated. There are tons of books on how to use your time, and the intent of this chapter is not to offer a scheduling tutorial. All I want to stress is that one fundamental activity in the Do realm is scheduling, or sending messages of availability.

Prioritizing

Reality is changing. Your universe is changing. What was important yesterday may not be so important today, or tomorrow. Prioritizing your doing means give room to what's important now as opposed to what you thought it was important yesterday. Prioritizing comes after scheduling and it's an important, often ignored part of the productivity process.

Prioritizing will conflict with scheduling and that's something normal. Prioritizing means giving space and energy to what's important now and reschedule what was left out. Many people get confused when they have to make changes based on the priority of the tasks but that's an important part of the Do realm.

How do you know what's important and what's not? Well, that is something you will have to micro Assess-Decide-Do every time. As I already mentioned, ADD is an abstract framework and supports any implementation you want. For instance, there will be a different prioritizing strategy in an ADD implementation for programming, than to an ADD implementations for relationships.

Finishing

If you start doing something, finish it. Or cut it out, if you can't do it anymore. As simple and dumb as it sounds, finishing is a very important part of the doing process. So important, that I felt the need to make it a separate process.

One of the most subtle yet powerful ways to procrastinate (like really procrastinate, loosing your time) is to remain stuck in a project or task for ever. There is this pressure not to finish the task, because... well, because you'll have to do something else. And you don't want. Or you are scared. Or bored. Or whatever.

I've been there so many times that I had to come up with a finishing strategy. I've been caught in so many situations where finishing seemed strange or inconvenient or not appropriate that I really had to reconsider all my attitude towards finishing. I'm sure you've been there: caught in a sticky relationship, in a never-ending project, in a just-above-the-fold job, and so on.

Finishing is the most important part of doing something. It frees your resources, it makes room for something new and it feeds the next Assess session. If you're not finishing what you're doing, you'll never be able to assess what you've done so far. Your ADD cycle will be stuck.

Creating Miracles

Doing is where the miracle takes place. By doing what you assessed and decided, you're changing your reality the way you want. Assessing is just a perspective and the decision is just an intention. If those are not backed up with constant activity and with real life actions, your Assess-Decide-Do cycle will be broken.

But if you're spending enough time in this cycle, if you succeed in Assessing, Deciding and Doing on a regular basis, if you engage totally in each part and let yourself flow freely through those stages, if you really become aware of the whole process, as simple and yet as powerful as it is, you're going to create miracles.

Starting with yourself.

FOCUS

In terms of Assess - Decide - Do, Focus is your capacity to be in only one realm at a certain moment. It's the measure of your atomic presence in each of these realms. Focus is also your reality creator. Everything which is not in your focus, doesn't really exist. It may be a mental construction somewhere in your head, but if you're not putting all your focus into it, it won't become alive. Now, the more focus you use, the more powerful your reality will be, right? And if you're dividing your focus you're dividing the force you put in creating your reality. I know it sounds a little bit pretentious, so let's try a little real life example here.

Let's say you're driving your car and at the same time you're wondering what to do when you're home. In this case you're focusing on (and at the same time, you're building) two realities: the reality in which you're driving your car and the reality in which you're doing something at home.

Physically, you're only on one reality and that's the one with your car. If your focus is not entirely there, that reality will weaken, and it will be much difficult to control it. You may lose the sense if immersion, the joy, the relaxation feelings. You can even lose the control of the car, leaving your reality at the mercy of somebody else.

The other reality that you feed with your focus, the "at home" reality is not very powerful yet. It's not in your physical reach right now so it can only be designed or planned. The most important fact about that reality is that it is a consequent reality of your car driving reality. It's coming after that, it depends on that. If you're not doing your current reality right, you can even lose the "at home" reality. Somebody else may run you over, if you're not driving carefully enough.

It's the same in every aspect of your life: if you're not totally immersed in your current reality you can't really create your future reality. If you're not fueling your immediate activities with all the available focus, that reality will weaken putting at risk every potential realities you can create from what you are. Putting your focus on different, parallel realities, as exciting as it might be, can jeopardize your current reality. Multi-tasking is a myth.

That's why being in only one realm at a certain moment is so important in Assess - Decide - Do. Too much mixing your presence in two or three realms at the same time not only it will weaken the overall structure of each, but it will also give much less force to anything you may want to build.

FLOW

Each time you're using your focus to assess, decide or do, you're doing it with a certain vibration. Flow is the aligned vibration with your current status.

Usually, there are very few situations in which you are completely immersed into assessment, decision or doing. Instead, you're mixing them in various quantities. You don't experience a complete flow from your assessment to the decision and from there to the doing. You are doing a partial assessment, a partial decision and from there emerges partial doing.

Flow is the degree at which you are using those states to create your reality. Each time you'll have a lower degree of alignment with your current status, your flow will be affected. You will be experiencing obstacles, difficulties, elasticity, inertia. Each time you have a higher degree of alignment with your current status you will be experiencing ease, openness, satisfaction and fulfillment.

As you may guess, flow is a function of your focus. The more you use your focus to atomically and totally explore each of those main states: assessment, decision and doing, the more you'll increase your flow.

Flow is not a measurable concept although we can refer to it as bigger, lower or we can define some quality of it. Flow is usually perceived as your capacity to enjoy and align with what you're doing. Most of what we call joy, happiness or exhilaration is in one way or another a definition of a great flow we're experiencing.

If focus will be the main tool for creating your reality we may refer to the flow as the master glue for keeping the pieces together. A healthy flow will allow you to go from a complete assessment to an atomic decision and that will lead to a totally immersed activity of doing.

ADD As An Object Oriented Paradigm

I'm going to tell you something I bet you didn't know about me: I majored in foreign languages, with a diploma in French literature, but I never practiced. I worked as a radio anchor for a few years and then started my own online publishing company. Circumstances forced me to learn programming by myself. As in many other areas, in programming I'm self-educated.

One of the most useful things I learned by being a programmer is something called "Object Oriented Programming". I'm not going to get very technical here, so don't run away. I promise there will be a meaningful connection between this out of the blue introduction and the main topic of this chapter. Also, apologies to those who are really good at programming for the following paragraph.

JUST A FEW LINES OF CODE

Object Oriented, often shortened as OOP, is a way to describe your application data. Let's say you're going to use a lot of geometrical forms in your application. Instead of creating Circles, Squares or Rectangles every time you need them, you create an abstract class, called, let's say GeometricalForms. You define a few properties for this class, like "shape", "color" and so on.

Now, every time you need to use a geometrical form in your app, you just subclass the GeometricalForm. Let's say you need a Circle. You write something like this:

myCircle = new GeometricalForm;

The magic happens when you add your own attributes to the abstract class. In this case, the "shape" attribute would be "round" and that will define a circle.

myCircle.shape = "round";

Every other characteristic of the abstract class are automatically inherited. And by subclassing the abstract class you can create a lot of derived data, putting your own touches to it, while still maintaining the initial structure. Neat, right?

Hope this wasn't as technical as you expected it to be. The bottom line is that these simple concepts, like abstract (or parent) class and inheritance, which are really simple to grasp, are creating a very productive programming paradigm. You usually are much faster in an OO paradigm and you can create a much cleaner code. Not the mention that a cleaner code will lead to a more stable application.

What was the meaning of these few lines of code? Well, you can apply this OO pattern to any area in your life. Instead of taking things for granted, think at them as they are an "abstract" class. Make your own version by inheriting from them and adding your own attributes.

Not only will it be much easier, but it will dissolve a lot of internal resistance. As long as you still add your own touches to whatever concepts or methodologies you are trying to create, they are a part of yourself. So the resistance should be considerably lower.

MAKE YOUR OWN ADD

Assess-Decide-Do should not be taken "as is". It should be modified to suit your needs. In many ways, this framework is like an abstract class that you can take and subclass it.

If there's some methodology for brainstorming that you feel it will fit into the "Assess" realm, use it. If there's some planning tools for the Decide part, just go ahead, use them.

The core part of the framework is that each realm must be used atomically, without too much mixing with other realms (preferably with no mixing at all) and that you should ensure a smooth transition from one realm to another. These are the "read-only" properties of the abstract class. The fundamental, non-modifiable traits of the main "object". For the rest, you can define whatever you want.

For instance, mixing GTD with the Do realm would actually be a very good idea. GTD is perfect for getting things done, right? Just don't focus exclusively on GTD, ignoring the other components of the abstract class, like Assess or Decide.

You can also implement Assess - Decide - Do in relationships, in business, in personal branding, in productivity. Put your own touches and keep in mind the "read-only" properties. A few chapters later I will give you some examples of Applied ADD.

Life Imbalances Explained

With ADD

We know now a little bit about our realms. Now let's see how we can explain life imbalances by malfunctions of each realm.

ANALYSIS PARALYSIS - TOO MUCH ASSESS

One of the most common assessing imbalances is the "analysis paralysis" syndrome. You keep thinking and thinking and don't do anything. You never move away from that realm, you never get to decide what to do with all the information that you gathered so far. All you do is crunch information, in the hope that at some point that information will be useful to you.

Being in the Assess realm is comforting. Because you don't have to take any action at all. There is no risk involved in crunching data or in day dreaming. But comfort is the enemy of evolution. It's just a disguised prison. A sweet one, but still a prison. Keeping yourself in this prison of comfort will make you feel good. But by being stuck on this non-action territory, you'll actually generate bad outcomes.

All the good things are happening in the discomfort zone, not in a comfortable space. You can't grow unless you take some risks. The risk of making a move, any move, is the smallest risk you can take. Step away from the regular day dreaming sessions and start cleaning up your house, for instance. Stop learning too much and decide to do something with what you have already. The benefits may be way bigger than you imagine.

I'm sure you've been in that place and not only once. Sitting and just pondering stuff will most likely protect your from any potentially risky activity. The bad news is that even if you do nothing, somebody else is going to do something to you. Assessing forever is another word for giving up control of your life to somebody else.

Another common assessing imbalance is the "I didn't know" excuse. You didn't know that your business was entering a crowded market so you went bankrupt in the first 6 months. Or you didn't know you're approaching an aggressive or lazy partner and your relationship is a mess now.

The "I didn't know" excuse usually appears after some disastrous results of a Do realm activity. It's there and only there that you realize you should have been more careful, or at least a little patient before moving so fast to the Decision realm.

If only you took some time to assess...

SOMEDAY SYNDROME - TOO MUCH DECIDE

The most common deciding imbalance is the "one day I'll have my own business" syndrome. In this case you took the decision but you aren't really doing anything to move further. Your decision is strong, you trust yourself and your hopes are high. But you're not doing anything, you just took a decision and never moved from there. Endless planning, obsessive scheduling but no real step ahead, no action, nothing.

I'm sure you know the type: "starting tomorrow I'll quit smoking". Or: "I'm going to be a millionaire, starting with the next week-end". Being stuck too much in the Decide realm will weaken the Do realm, the one that should naturally flow from the decision. If all your focus is kept in Decide, you won't have any energy left for Do, obviously.

Another deciding imbalance is very close to shyness: I'm not going to do this, because "it won't matter anyway". Or because I will feel terribly bad if everybody will look at me while doing it. Your assessment was complete, you moved to the point where you can actually start doing it, but you decided to quit.

The Decide realm is a little bit privileged (and you'll see that more clearly in the iPhone app) because it offers 2 choices: you can move to Do, or just get back to Assess. You're free NOT to do something, and return it to Assess. But sticking too much stuff into Decide will eventually clog it.

Productivity Obsession - Too Much Do

The most common doing imbalance is the obsessed productivity freak. The guy that does stuff without thinking, just to be able to check some tasks done. This is the biggest productivity trap you can ever hit, and I saw quite often many promising careers falling down because of this. Just doing, without assessing and making the right decisions is a sure path to the underground world of the "still smiling but completely burned down inside" people.

Productivity is not the ability to do things efficiently. It's the ability to have a real life while doing things efficiently. There's no use in being completely dried out inside by the age of 40, but being a super effective top manager, spending you huge salary on life coaches and expensive trips just to alleviate the disastrous effects of the depression. Yes, focusing too much on Do has this effect.

Every Do task should be somehow fed back to the Assess realm. The Do realm is not the end of something, it's the beginning of another cycle. Hoping you'll be in for some treat if you spend all your time and life in the Do realm is plain dumb. The "Do" realm obsessed people are also those who are in love with crossing tasks off of their lists. Killing another task here, man I feel good. We'll talk down the line about the death of the deadline as we know it, but for now, let's take a look at assess-decide-do relationship with the attention deficit disorder and then try some practical exercises.

Assess - Decide - Do and Attention Deficit Disorder

I have to tell you that in my initial book structure there wasn't a chapter about this topic. It was added with just a few weeks before the launch. As I started to talk with my friends about this framework, they kept saying me there "must be a hidden link" between the initials of my framework and the Attention Deficit Disorder syndrome.

I had to ponder this for a while. At the first glance, this is a coincidence. I didn't have any intention whatsoever to target this exact sequence of letters. It just happened. The only problem is I don't believe in coincidences. Maybe my friends saw something. I don't have ADD (or at least not in a certified way, by a doctor) but I know there are moments in which I tend to drift away. I lose my focus.

Since I implemented Assess - Decide - Do in my life, meaning during the last year, those moments changed. I still have them, but somehow, my reaction towards them changed. I know that those escapes are just part of the Assess realm. I guess I somehow eliminated the guilt related to them. I don't think in terms "I just lose my time here" if I'm not doing something productive. I'm mentally using something like: "ok, I feel the need to assess this a little bit more".

Since I started to use Assess - Decide - Do I became insanely productive. Although I don't feel like a productivity "athlete", on the contrary, I feel pretty relaxed and flowing. But if I look at the rough reality I cannot ignore the fact that I did incredibly more than I usually do.

For instance, I started 2 live workshops, each with at least 2 reruns.

I published 4 ebooks in a month on Amazon, using CreateSpace (and those books are actually selling).

I grew my blog from 1000 subscribers a year ago to a steady 4000+ subscribers (at the moment of writing).

I released 2 free ebooks with hundreds and thousands of downloads.

I created an iPhone app in 30 days and that iPhone app is in the AppStore, actually on sale.

And is not only about work here. During the last year I started to understand and solve a lot of hidden problems in my personal life. It isn't the time and the place to name them here, but compared with the years before, last one was an incredible breakthrough.

Now, there must be something good here. As always, I encourage you to take it for a dry test and see if it works for you. Don't take my words for granted. Assess for yourself.

Also, keep in mind that I'm not a qualified doctor. I don't know if Assess - Decide - Do will at least alleviate your ADD symptoms, but I do know it worked for me, in a very constant, powerful and effective way.

Part Two: Applied ADD

ADD for Relationships

We're social animals. We cannot function outside relationships, outside a social paradigm in which we interact with other individuals. Quite often, when you read something about relationships, it's about couple relationships. But the fact is we have far more interactions than our love relationships, and this chapter will be geared towards this more general perception of relationships. It's true, love affairs are quite close to our emotional being, so we tend to give them precedence. Sometimes by ignoring other types of relationships.

Your social behavior is sculpted by everything you do, with everybody, not only your couple relationship. It really doesn't matter if you have a great couple thing, if you're socially impaired. And it wouldn't help you much to be the funniest guy at all parties, if you can't settle in a long term relationship. Besides living in a couple, there are many other levels of social life: friendship, relatives, work, incidental relationships.

The goal is to have a consistent relationship approach to everything, not just to your intimate behavior. Creating a manageable approach to every single interaction is what gives you balance, not excellence in one single area.

Assess For Relationships

The first thing you have to assess when you're in a relationship (again, being it a couple relationship, a friends relationship or a work relationship) is its dual nature. There are always two levels:

- you, as individuals
- relationship, as an entity

The way you interact as individuals is one thing, but your relationship expands beyond this. The relationship as a single entity has an impact on the outside world. Every single action inside this relationship will create something outside the reach of each of you.

There is no 1 + 1 = 2 in relationships. It's always 1 + 1 = more.

ENERGY EXCHANGE

Another key point in assessing a relationship is the energy exchange: do I give? and do I receive? You can give a lot of stuff: your time, your money, your knowledge, or you can just give love. It really depends on what type of relationship this is. For instance, if you're having a working relationship, you're giving both time and knowledge. If it's a friendship relationship, you're giving your time, your understanding, your listening capabilities and love. And perhaps some more.

The same goes with what you receive. You can receive money, time, knowledge, experience. Or, of course, love. If it's a working relationship you receive most of the time, money and experience. If it's a friendship relationship you receive understanding, guidance, compassion or love.

The biggest obstacle for assessing the existence of a real energy exchange is the status quo. You may think: "well, he was always my friend, even if I don't get much out of this relationship". Or: "We're married, what more can I expect?". Or: "I'm not getting too much out of this job relationship, but I cannot change it". Status quo is the biggest enemy of your relationship, because it makes you keep that relationship going, even if the energy exchange is not there anymore. If you can't challenge your relationship at least every 6 months, you're in a status quo.

The thought that you may get something unpleasant out of this assessment may also make you avoid the whole process: better stay as you are than to realize you're not well.

Hopefully, applying an ADD approach will make things a little bit easier. You're in the Assess realm, and one of the most important characteristics of the Assess realm is that you don't have to decide or do anything. The Assess realm is giving you the freedom to see things as they are, without taking a decision. You may stay in the Assess realm as long as you want, without deciding anything, if you don't want it.

IS THIS BETTER OR WORSE?

Another thing you will usually do while in the Assess realms is what I call the quality assessment, an evaluation of what makes you better – or worse, for what it matters – by staying in that relationship. It's a very important assessment, and it's usually the very next after the energy exchange check. Since you already had an energy exchange, and decide it to pursue it, now let's see if it's good or not.

It will depend a lot on your personal values system, so there's no rule that says: "this will be good for your relationship". I don't encourage anyone to buy ready-made opinions about what is good or bad about them. Instead, I encourage people to think for themselves and reach to their own conclusions.

Knowing if you're getting something good or bad out of your relationship can be difficult. Things are changing, you are changing, the partner is changing. What was ok yesterday may not be ok today. Will see more about the time constraint in the next paragraph, but until then, let's note that it's very important to find a way to realize if it's good or bad for you.

As a rule of thumb, if you can be relaxed in a relationship, this is usually a sign of positive energy exchange. If you're uptight and feel pressure, probably you're getting some bad vibes. But there are exceptions to this: for instance, if you're having a challenging partner at work, that means you can learn and grow faster, although it will cost you a little stress. And you can feel relaxed in the company of a deceiving person who's trying to fool you. It's really your job to see if you're getting something valuable or not.

THE TIME CONSTRAINT

Is this relationship temporary? Is this going to last more than a night, or a train conversation, or a temporary assignment? There are a lot of relationships modifiers based on how long the relationship have to last.

If you're having a conversation with somebody you don't know, about a problem you must solve, this is going to last until the problem is solved, no more. From several minutes to several hours or days. It will require a different amount of commitment than a relationship meant to last for a year.

I consider the time constraint very important in assessing a relationship because we tend to act on auto-pilot: we learned several approaches and we tend to apply them without thinking too much. So, we end up giving too much attention and commitment to insignificant relationships, while ignoring other, allegedly more important ones.

Let me explain: if you have a relationship at work with somebody who's repairing your computer, you don't have to give him flowers at the end of the job. A simple "thank you" will be enough. But you may want to give flowers to your wife every other day, in order to feed a longer relationship. We tend to take the longest relationships for granted, while new, intriguing things are far more appealing. Taking those intriguing relationships through the time constraint always puts me on the right track.

Decide For Relationships

As you may already have guessed, this is not a guide on which decision you have to make in order to improve your relationships. It's more like a general approach, leaving the implementation details up to you. However, there are some things which are specific to relationships, things which can dramatically improve the effects of any decision, making it work faster or deeper.

TRANSPARENCY

Whatever decision you're taking, in a relationship this must be transparent. It's so simple, yet so often forgotten. It comes down to this simple word: "talk". Talk with the partner about your decision, talk about what made you took the decision, talk about the effects of that decision.

If you're not transparent about your decisions, you can't have a relationship. It's simple: if the other one is not aware of what are you up to, he can't help you. Can't disturb you either, that's true, but that's exactly what I said: this isn't a relationship anymore.

Lack of transparency is very often the root cause of any bad relationship. Being it an intimate relationship, a friendly one or a work relationship. Just talk it out loud.

CHALLENGE

Another specific point in the Decide realm for relationships is that your decision will be most likely challenged. The other one will hear you — if you were transparent about the decision, of course — and will respond. Sometimes will agree, sometimes not. That's the nature of a relationship, there is more than one person in it and in order to function properly, everyone must agree.

If you're a strong headed individual, that will hurt. Having your decision challenged can be a real pain if you're not used to it. But once accepted, the benefits of this constant challenge will be fantastic: you'll actually start to function on a new level, in a relationship. You'll become part of something bigger than you, no matter the type of the relationship.

If you're not having your decisions challenged, the relationship is either not working, or not worth continuing.

Do For Relationships

Again, the Do realm won't teach you how to make a friend from your boss or how to avoid a weekly fight with your wife. You're already smart enough for that. But it will show you instead some of the subtle differences of the Do realm when it comes to relationships, as opposed to other areas of your life.

DOING MEANS RECEIVING

Whatever you chose to do in your relationship, there will always be a receiving part of it. Since you're in a relationship, you're not only giving, you're receiving too. The energy exchange you identified in the Assess realm will still be active in the Do realm, so better take it into account.

Like the transparency thing, this is also forgotten big time. One must be prepared to receive as well as to give. Not receiving from the other part (not listening, not doing required stuff, not accepting gratitude or love) will block and eventually drain the energy exchange.

DOING MEANS COMPLETING

In a relationship you're going to support, more than achieve. As an individual, you're mostly achieving things, but in a relationship you're forming alliances, you're creating shared values, you're implementing strategies. Keep in mind that whatever you're doing, in a relationship your actions must complete the actions of the other partners, in order to have a working environment.

This comes often to a sense of oneness, a higher level of human interaction. Relationships are born from a need and as you're satisfying your needs through that relationship (security needs, emotional needs, material needs) the other part must do this too. Whatever you do, keep in mind the other and his needs.

***

As you can see, in this ADD exercise, the biggest part is the Assess one. It's not a surprise, since many relationships are broken because of hasty decisions or immaturity, which are both signs of an incomplete Assess realm.

Assessing what you're giving and receiving through the energy exchange and putting it into a time perspective is not rocket science. They are simple actions which can be converted to habits and streamline your relationships approach. Other key points are that every decision will be transparent (must be, since it will affect other persons) and challenged. In the Do realm, expect to receive from and to complete your partners.

ADD for Dealing With Interruptions

I know you've been there. Interruptions can be caused by working in a stressful environment with lots of interactions, or by yourself as a self made interruption reflex. One of the most common reflexes for creating self-made interruptions is social media. Checking up your status or timeline a few times per day. Or per hour. Or per minute.

They may be the results of a stressful environment or of your own habit, either way, interruptions are not a healthy thing. Or, to be more clear, are not managed, traditionally, in a healthy way. How can ADD help here?

First of all, an ADD implementation for dealing with interruptions will have to put the interruption into the Assess realm. Most of the time, you're in the Do, "doing" something, and somebody interrupts you. Well, you tend to incorporate that interruption in the same realm, into Do. You follow up without assessing, either by immersing in that new task, either by rejecting it completely (can't you see I'm busy here?).

Putting the interruption in the Assess realm will have an immediate effect: you will not follow up immediately, instead, you will analyze the interruption. Is it critical? Is it important? Can be postponed? Can be done in a reasonable amount of time without shifting your focus too much? After the assessment, you move it to Decide. If the decision is to follow up, you establish a context and a time and move it to Do. If the context is "where I am right now" and the time is "right now" it means you're following up with the interruption.

But there are a few subtle things that happened in the background of this whole process. First of all, you may not assign a context or a time to the interruption at all. You can just acknowledge and move on. That will make the interruption stay in the Assess. For instance, if a colleague is asking something from you that you can't or don't want to provide at the moment, you just acknowledge and move on. "I can't answer this right now". This is a valid response.

Second, you may establish a context and a time which is not in the current time/space continuum. You may say: "Ok, I decided to follow up on this, at my Office, tomorrow". Now you can get back to work, the interruption has been through Assess and Decide, but didn't made it to the current Do. It will be of course, in tomorrow's Do, but that's only tomorrow. Now you can get back to work.

Applying ADD, specifically moving an interruption to Assess from the Do, has an interesting effect. You will soon become actually interested in them, in a certain way. You will see what I mean in the next paragraph. Somehow, by acknowledging the fact that you're not forced to Do something about an interruption, you will not be afraid of them anymore. On the contrary, you will start to pay more attention to what comes to your focus, because, as I said, in a strange way, those interruption can be beneficial too.

Interruptions Are Not Toxic

They're only horrendously managed. Most of the time, it's true, you will get interruptions that will tend to shift your focus in a destructive way.

But there are a few times when you will be happy to be interrupted. When a new idea came into your head, for instance. Admit it, there is no time when you sit still and ideas are popping into your head, disciplined and organized. Any idea is in fact an interruption in your normal workflow. If you go implement it immediately or discard it immediately, meaning if you're going to keep in Do, you will lose it. But if you Assess it, the worst thing that may happen is that you will have a reference of it in your Assess realm. It will be there. You will know that at some point you had an idea, but never made any decision about it.

So, the old, traditional way of "blocking as many interruptions as you can" may not be always beneficiary.

In short, here's how a standard management of an interruption will be with ADD:

If you're interrupted, don't fight it:

1. Assess: is it worth keeping it? Discard it? Brainstorm it?

2. Decide: if it's going to stay, sign a time/space contract with it: here and now, or tomorrow at noon

3. Do it: do it, or re-Decide it.

As simple as that.

Personal Crisis
Management With ADD

Crisis management is a delicate topic. Crises are unpleasant, and crisis management is designed specifically to ease the pain and to help with the side effects. Since crisis management is such a large topic, I decided to focus only on personal crisis here, although you can apply this to larger groups or communities too.

It's Not A Crisis, It's A Result

The first and most important part of an ADD evaluation of a crisis is acceptance. The situation you are in, as painful as it may be, is just a result of something. You're there because you applied, at some point, an ADD cycle that proved to generate unhappy consequences.

If you can look at things like that, you will be forced to answer a very important question: is this really a crisis, or the result of your conscious choices? We tend to perceive crisis like a disruptive process, like something that tears down our entire existence, but this perception in itself may be misleading. Most of the time we do live in an incongruent world, but we keep telling to ourselves that the world is congruent. We try to project a sense of security over it, maintaing some status quo. Until a certain event forces us to look at the world exactly how it is.

Accepting the fact that a personal crisis is the result of your own choices will force you to stay in Assess, rather than trying to Do something about the crisis. And that's the best thing you can do about it, so to speak. Many times, in a desperate tentative of "getting out of the crisis" we perform the exact sequence of tasks which brought us in the very place of the disasters. We may only change the actors and places, but we repeat the same mistakes over and over again.

Placing yourself in the Assess realm in the middle of a personal crisis is difficult in the beginning. Your familiar universe is crumbling over you and you feel the urge to run away, to protect yourself. The fight or flight response will try to force you to avoid thinking and choose survival. It's tough to stop and think when you're hit. But then again, if you don't stop, you may rush into the exact same situation as before.

So, take the time to think things over. What you experience right now may look like something that hit you out of the blue, but it isn't. At some point, you did something that created that. Find out what it was.

Most of the time, the result of the Assessment in a personal crisis ends up with two types of results:

- What you did was a mistake, and you experience the consequences
- What you did wasn't wrong, but you are still experiencing some bad results: so you're having some growth pains

For instance, if you're experiencing massive financial stress, this may be for two reasons: you either didn't spend your money well (or didn't make any, for what matters) or you did spend it well, but the refill rate is slower than you anticipated.

In the first case, you did something wrong and you're experiencing the consequences. You didn't manage your financial situation correctly.

In the second case, you managed it well, the money will eventually come, but you have to learn something out of it. It may be that you have to learn something about the money making process, like making it faster or in a more streamlined way. Or it may be something related to your own expectations, you may have to learn how to align your expectations with the time / space constraint of your actions.

Either way, the financial crisis is the result of your own conscious acts.

Once you understand what happened exactly, move to Decide.

The Decision: Make A New Space/Time Projection Of Yourself

Once you understand the reasons for your situation, it's time to step out of it. But you must take care of the decision. You must project a very clear time / space projection of your future self. It doesn't suffice to keep saying motivating stuff and to think positively. It may alleviate some pains, but thinking positively in a crisis situation without having a clear image of Where and When you want to be, is plain useless.

The Decision in a personal crisis starts with a new you. Put this new image of you in a new time and space continuum. Something like: "In 3 months I will have my debt reduced with 50%, I will have a new job and a new apartment". That's a correct and easy to understand Decision when you're in a personal financial crisis. The same type of decision may apply to a personal relationship crisis: "In 3 months I will live alone, in a new place".

The Decide realm is the place where you project your outcome. This is where your intention is made clear and the whole Do process will follow exactly what you Decide here.

Many personal crisis are reloaded again and again by lack of a correct Decision. Suppose you already Assessed what went wrong. But when it comes to Decision, most of the time you want to rewind the time to the moment before the actions that drove you to that crisis and nothing more. That will not work. Even more, it will put you in a very favorable context of doing the same mistake again.

A correct decision must take into account that you live now, not in the past, and you act in a certain context, which is here, not somewhere else. If you assessed that you're experiencing growth pains, this approach is easier to understand: you're actually in a learning process.

But even if you assessed that you made some mistakes, try to incorporate the past experience into this decision. This and only this will prevent your from making the same mistake again.

What Do You Do In A Personal Crisis?

The short version: you Do exactly what you Decided. The long version: you lose some parts of your life and at the same time you try to insert some new parts into your life. Sounds much easier than it actually is, and I'm aware of that.

The most difficult part in a personal crisis management is the Do part. You may develop some patience and a sense of presence so you will won't rush directly into Do, choosing to Assess first. You may also incorporate the experience from what went wrong and make the right Decision. But the Do part is where you actually make things happen.

And I agree it's tough. But it's tough anyway, even if you use, or don't use ADD. In the latest case, at least you'll have a clearer perspective of what went wrong and where do you want to be now. It may not be the best Decision and your implementation may suck, again. But now all you have to do is to move to Assess again and start over.

ADD and Inbox Zero

As a long time GTD'er, I was always concerned about the size of my "inbox". Those of you familiar with the methodology know what I'm talking about. The less items you have in your inbox, the better you're supposed to feel. And you get to have less items in your Inbox by processing them. I confess this was a very valuable lesson for me and for a while, a solid principle to follow. I think I processed constantly my inboxes for at least 2 years.

But, from a certain point, I didn't feel like having an Inbox zero anymore. I couldn't say it was a sudden realization, it just happened. I'm sure that for a while I continued to use the GTD principles and, as I already said, I do think GTD is a very good tool, but only in the Do realm. But then, again, we're not existing only in the Do realm, we're spending time in Assess and Decide as well. Fact is that my Inbox started to enjoy a few extra items all the time. Surprisingly, I didn't feel bad at all. On the contrary.

So, after a few months of constantly using ADD, while at the same time slowly getting over the GTD habits, I realized what happened. There were 2 things: first, there was the concept of Inbox that was challenged, and then it was a big incongruence between GTD and ADD. These two events made me quit the zero Inbox gang. Let's look at those two major breakthroughs with a little more attention.

First of all, in ADD you don't have inboxes, in the traditional productivity sense. Assess, Decide and Do are not inboxes, they are levels of commitment. That's a fundamental difference. In each realm you're performing with a certain focus energy and each realm actually needs some objects in it, otherwise, your focus couldn't hang on anything. So, having items in my Assess, Decide and Do realms was the best thing that could happen to me. An Inbox zero was inconceivable under these new circumstances.

Second, the only thing that could remotely look like an Inbox was the Assess realm, but by definition, that realm could not be zero. Assess is the unique entry point in your system, it's the only place when you allow new information to reach you. If you have no things left to

Assess in your life, you have two options: either start enjoying Nirvana, because you're already there, or check your pulse and see if you're still living. Again, a zeroed Inbox was totally against the framework rules.

So, the major shift in my paradigm was not only to reconsider the whole definition of an Inbox, but also the fact that having items to do is a sign of being a valid person. An Inbox is not an inbox anymore, it's just a level of commitment. Commitment to Assess, Decide or Do something that is already there.

We're not just recipients of information hitting us randomly and transforming us into task performers. We're far more than that. We can Decide on that information and we can also implement it, Do the task. So, every time we perform in any of these realms, we have a certain level of commitment to them. We process pieces of information and send them from one realm to another. That's what we're supposed to do. Not to empty them. In the next chapter, you'll see that this "emptying" approach, along with the word "deadline" can create a really disempowering attitude.

And then, the fact that you have stuff to act on in these realms, or in other words, the fact that you have to Do what you Assessed and Decided to, well, that's incredibly refreshing. You're going to see down the road, in the third part of the book, that in my app, I have 3 realms with badge numbers of them. Every time I didn't see a number on a badge (meaning there were no items left to Assess, Decide or Do), I was like freaking out. Wait: I don't have anything to Assess? Nothing to Decide upon? That's strange...

Having things to do is a proof that I'm still alive. It's also a proof that I already Assessed them and Decided to go on Doing them. Whatever appears in my Do realm was a function of my own input filters and was a personal choice. As such, is an act of happiness to immerse in my Do realm, creating my own planned miracles.

The more, the better.

The Death Of The Deadline As We Know It

I was a big fan of deadlines. Chasing them. Crossing them off of my todo list. Striving to meet them. Spending countless hours just to prepare myself for this date with my deadline. Oh, the feeling of pride when I was there in time to make it. The inner power and fulfillment... Yes, that was a very interesting experience.

I'm not into deadlines anymore but I do remember the feeling of satisfaction I got from crossing my deadlines off. I still enjoy doing things, I'm just not into deadlines anymore. As simple as it seems, this is a fundamental difference.

The Word

Have you ever really thought what is the meaning of the word "deadline"? It has the word "death" in it. Never wondered why? Because a deadline is a line of death. Once you meet that line, you kill the task. You take its life away. You conquered it. You extended your presence onto its territory, occupied it and now you have the right to eliminate it from your system. That's a highly motivating psychology. Also, it's a very disempowering one.

Thinking in terms of "death" lines will make you assimilate the end of a task with its death. Doing things will mean kill one task after another. Slashing tasks over a to do list has this feeling of power: I killed 32 enemies today, I feel good. Tasks are not your enemy. Nobody is, in fact. You just pretend that they are, so you can use the "warrior" resources you already have deep down in your ancestral behavior. The pressure of doing more and more exalted our warrior style way over the safety level.

We position ourselves as conquerors of our own task land. What lies in front of our work day is a field filled with enemies that have to be eliminated. Every day is a battle. Many productivity techniques are using this subliminal approach. What you have to do is a burden. You have to take it away, to overcome it, to eliminate it.

The more you eliminate, the better you'll feel. Train yourself to become better at killing tasks.

At a certain level, this psychology is, as I already said, very motivating. Fighting for our survival is deeply wired in our unconscious memory. This is why we find it easy to understand this approach. Fear of our own death will push us to kill the "other". And the "other" in this case, is clearly written on our daily to do list. If we don't kill "them", they will kill us, so we'd better jump off of our beds, rush into the subway and take position in our daily trenches, suitably camouflaged as desks.

But the downside of this, its disempowering part, is that by transforming your tasks into your personal enemies, you'll eventually become so good at deadlines that life itself will look as a deadline. You'll rush towards the biggest deadlines of all: your own death. Deadline by deadline, task killed by task killed, you're going to eventually cross the final episode off of your to do list with great satisfaction. The ultimate project management victory: I solved my own death today.

For A Liveline Philosophy

Forget deadlines. Instead let's have livelines. A liveline is different from a deadline in that it creates a new starting point. The point where you start something on the foundation you just finished, something alive. You restart the movement.

In Assess - Decide - Do, your tasks will always generate a new cycle. You're not spending time only in Do. You're also spend time in Assess or in Decide. Each time you finish a task in Do, you will have to feed your Assess realm with the results. You will evaluate feedback. In this respect, a project is never "finished" in ADD. The graphical representation of a project in Assess - Decide - Do will look more like a spiral than like a Gantt diagram. I agree it's a little difficult to understand this concept, especially if you're coming from a long traditional task management experience.

A liveline will never ask you to cross a task over. You always have the possibility to re-start the liveline by sending it back to Decide, and, from there, back to Assess. A liveline will be met only if all the initial stages are completed and fulfilled. And every liveline will generate in turn several ideas, lessons or potential tasks.

A liveline means we're taking the "death" out of the deadline. We're taking the pressure out, we're taking the urge of finishing it so we can get back to our regular life. Because there will be no dichotomy between what you "have" to do and your regular life. It will all take place in the same time/space continuum.

I hear you loud and clear: what about commitments? What about promises? What about our corporate life where we have to finish tasks before competition, otherwise we're out of business? Well, if you do establish a certain end date to a task, keep it. It means you Assessed it right and you also took the right Decision about it. If you spent enough time in those two realms, nothing can go wrong.

Every Do imbalance is in fact a liability you carry on from the previous realms. If you can't finish a task in the specified time and space constraints, it means something went wrong on the Assess and Decide realms. Completing a task is not just a function of the Do, it's also a function of Assess and Decide. Until you realize that it will be really difficult to understand the benefits of the Assess - Decide - Do framework.

How about "unexpected" events? Let's say you did your best in Assess to anticipate every possible outcome and you properly allocated time and space resources in Decide. And still, some catastrophe happened. A power outage 2 hours before the client presentation or a traffic jam which delayed your presence at that important meeting. Well, things are happening. It doesn't mean you're off track. Back to Assess.

In a traditional approach, you would consider the undone task a liability. In the best case, you would have tried to reschedule or postpone. Meaning you would still keep yourself in the Do realm. Stuck on the deadline. And for as long as you're stuck in the same mindset, the problem will never disappear.

Take a leap of faith. Go out. Make a lateral step. Transform that deadline into a liveline. A liveline will give you flexibility not only at the action level, but also at the perception level. Start assessing what went "wrong" and see what could you've done better. There are many reasons for why you can't really Do a thing. Keeping yourself only in Do will hide those details, will lock you in the Do box. You can't see the real picture if you're not taking time to assess.

Perhaps the presentation wasn't ready. Perhaps the client wasn't ready to receive your message. Perhaps the meeting wasn't very good for your career. There are so many things you should ponder about what's happening around you and still, because you're pressuring on Do, you skip them. Or you avoid them consciously because they won't "help" you in any way.

Inject Some Life Into That Deadline

And make it a liveline. By now, you should understand that there is a little bit of a word game here: dead versus alive. I deliberately pushed the comparison a little bit. Of course you will commit to doing things in Assess - Decide - Do too. Of course you will do the best to meet your own expectations, at least. What's different, though, from the traditional productivity approach, is an unprecedented degree of flexibility.

In a traditional approach, if something went wrong, you would at best re-schedule and try to refill the Do realm with that task. Or lose it all together. In Assess-Decide - Do, you will reintroduce the task into your Assess realm. Of course you can just Re-Decide it, and in many day by day circumstances, that would be the expected reaction, but you also have another realm to work with, Assess.

I will avoid using a term like "planning" when it comes to Assess. You do much more than planning. You evaluate, you imagine, you wait, you dream about it, you play with the task as in a dream world. The degree of flexibility offered by the mere idea that you can be productive while Assessing is incredible.

And finally, one of the most important benefits of this bouncing back and forth is the organic rearrangement of your activity. Projects, tasks and events will start to fall into their places. The initial feeling will be one of melting, of losing control. But after this rather scary period, another feeling will come into place: the feeling of flow. There is an inner capacity of natural order, of simple flow from one project to another.

The deadline carries with it a threat. If you won't do it, something or somebody must die. In 99.99% of the cases, the task will die, and you will actually kill it. But a liveline will not have any threat associated. It's like "doing nothing" and yet "doing it". A good deal of resistance to implementing Assess - Decide - Do will come, ironically, from the fact that you associate "doing" things with pressure. And when you're not feeling pressure you're going to feel like you're doing nothing. If there's no deadline it means there's nothing to do, right? Wrong. you can do things in the absence of a deadline, just by knowing that the results will not get lost in a to do planner, but they'll be part of a bigger, flexible system that you can work with. I know, you associated doing with pressure. But no, with a liveline there is no pressure. And you can still do things.

Now, I hear you for the final question: are one going to do more using Assess - Decide - Do than using any other productivity framework? My answer to this question will always be: "more" is not automatically "better". The consumerist obsession put a lot of weight on "more". If you live in the deprivation of only one realm, spending your entire life in the Do realm, "more" becomes important. "More" is a way of measuring what you're Doing. But once you get out of the prison of Doing, spending time in Assess and Decide, "more" will lose its meaning as a measurement tool. It will be only a choice, an assessment. I can Do more today, or I can spend more time Deciding or Assessing.

ADD - Natural Productivity

Natural productivity means having a life while still doing what is important for you to do.

If you look carefully at the meaning of the word "productivity" you'll see there is nothing natural about productivity as an activity. Productivity is a term for machines. They have to perform in certain parameters and they have to deliver certain results. We, humans, we don't have to do that. We don't have to do anything, after all. We're here to live, not to be productive.

At some point in our life, we may decide, however, that we should perform in a certain way. That we want to follow some dreams, to implement some actions. To obtain a certain result. In that case, we should consider a certain consistency of our actions, a certain model of our day to day tasks, in such a way that we will obtain what we wanted. This is natural productivity. A certain glue between our much more sensitive and unexplainable part, and the power of our intentions and doing.

We're supposed to dream, otherwise, we wouldn't have this ability. We're supposed to imagine new things, to just observe our reality without modifying it or to just sit and evaluate our environment. That's natural productivity too. That's a part of our existence here that should be taken into account somehow. We can't isolate it from what were Doing.

We need a bigger, more consistent model for managing our lives. We need a way to accept the fact that we're not robots, implementing programs. And still, we need to perform like robots, if need be. And if we consciously choose it.

Traditional productivity is expressed through Gantt diagrams. Milestones, deadlines and resource allocation. Natural productivity is expressed as a spiral. You approach your goal in smaller and smaller circles, taking into account all the new information that you obtain after you finished some parts of it. And at the same time, by incorporating this new knowledge, you grow, you climb. You're not going horizontal, milestone by milestone, in a dumb, monotonous and stupid march. You're evolving.

Traditional productivity took away a core part of our human beings, and that is trust. Why would you create such perfect plans and strategies to implement something, why would you think at every possible obstacle and put into a fool-proof system, up to the point the system will perform almost on auto-pilot? Because you don't trust you can do it. I know it sounds esoteric and a little bit pretentious, but if you really take a step back, you'll understand that every productivity technique is in fact a replacement for our lost trust in our capacity of creating what we want.

As such, traditional productivity aimed to create the shortest, the most automated path from what we want to what we get. The shortest, most simple and accurate line you can imagine. Unfortunately, the Universe in which we live is not like that. It's not simple, it's not accurate and it's not predictable. The more efforts we put into controlling the processes, the more power we lose. And the results are not even remotely worth the effort. The smallest perturbation will throw us off the fixed track in a second. And then we re-start the same tedious process of establishing deadlines, allocating resources and so on.

Fact is we need a system in which we should take into account the entropy. A system which should be comfortable to the randomness or lack of meaning of some events in our lives. A system which could function in an understandable way, but which should also accept the fact that sometimes we don't need deadlines. That sometimes we need more info on a certain topic. That we have to re-decide parts of our tasks, projects or lives, without the guilt of "starting over".

And make this in a formalized, implementable way.

It will be a little difficult to implement ADD in the beginning. We're not used to have such a certain degree of trust in our capacities. We need something much more coercible and strict. ADD is not like this. It has an unprecedented degree of flexibility. This is why ADD is primarily a life management framework and not a productivity technique.

And yet, by allowing ourselves to move away from Assess to Decide and from there to Do, by giving ourselves this freedom to be in each of them atomically and follow this process back and forth for as many times as we need to properly align to our real desires, we could attain a whole new level in productivity.

Here are some of the most obvious benefits of ADD.

1. Eliminate The Deadline Guilt

As you already read, there are no deadlines in ADD, there are only livelines. Each result of a task can, and will, in most cases, feed a new cycle. If you finished the action, you'll get some feedback that you'll have to Assess. If you chose to Re-Decide that action, you'll "sign a new contract" to it. The more you Re-Decide, the better you become at the whole process.

You start to learn a lot of stuff about yourself. Maybe you aren't such a good doer, and need some help? Maybe you have the "Someday Syndrome"? Maybe you're an incurable dreamer? If you're only chasing deadlines, you can't learn any of the above. You can only experience a "warrior" style victory over a finished task, or experience some guilt for not doing that task.

By looking at this whole process from a circular point of view, you will start to identify where are the weak parts of your activity. And you can start to improve, using the same framework: Assess - Decide - Do. The only thing that will disappear will be the guilt from not doing something. Because you've now taken care of it.

2. Incorporate Procrastination

Every time you feel the urge to just let your thoughts run away, there's something pressuring you not to. You're not allowed to do that. This is procrastination. It's forbidden. And yet, our capacity of day dreaming is a fundamental piece of our creativity. We have a really hard time doing things that we didn't "see" before in in our mind. If we imagined them before, it's much easier.

This role is fulfilled by the Assess realm. This is where you're allowed to dream, to brainstorm, to play roles, to drift away. You're allowed to. That's why it exists. The moment a piece of information requires a decision, the moment you can't add something to, or assess anything about it, that piece of information will be moved to Decide.

In a traditional productivity approach, procrastinating should be avoided as being "toxic". Because it keeps you from "doing" things. Well, in ADD, there's no limit to the things you can imagine, dream, or brainstorm. As long as you understand that this is all you do in that realm. And that you should move away from it, not to the Do, instantly, but to the Decide realm. The place where you should decide what to do with what you dreamed.

3. Endless Projects

In traditional productivity a project has a start date and an end date. The "spiral" nature of ADD will kinda invalidate this model. In ADD a project is really endless. Some parts of it may be crossed off, may be finished, consumed. But every consumed action will feed back the Assess realm and it will generate another idea. An idea that could stay there for as long as it needed until a decision is made.

Although it seems a little scary, it isn't. The rejection feeling you had when you read the "endless projects" words is just a reminiscence of your traditional productivity patterns. You think in terms of milestones and deadlines, you see the world in a discontinuous way. In fact, the world is in continuous and unceasing movement. Start and end are just artificial conventions for us to isolate in time some processes.

Working with endless projects means you'll be in the normal flow of the things. The end of something will be the beginning of something else. In a very clear and natural way.

4. Learning By Doing

In ADD you will re-evaluate your skills and capacities continuously. You will be forced by the framework to do that. If you enter a relationship, for instance, and you had an incomplete Assessment, at some point something in Do will force you to go back. Ok, where I am now? What am I doing wrong? Something will have to be re-assessed and a new Do stage will have to start.

The same thing will happen in a much more mundane territory like work. If you start a project, you don't have to worry that you have an incomplete research, as long as you have the drive and the available time and space resources to Decide on that project. You start and at some point you will have to get back. That's learning by doing in the most simple and effective way.

This is exactly what I did when I started to code my own iPhone app for this framework (the technical details are on the next chapters, by the way). I started with the drive to create a minimum product demo, to see how the framework works in real life and I didn't have any Objective C expertise at all. But every time I hit a roadblock, I went back and re-started the whole process. Sometimes I spent a few hours per day only in Assess, reading, learning and crunching information. Some other times I just coded the entire day, Doing stuff.

You'll be the judge of the result, by the way, because what follows is the third, and last part of this ebook, when I'm going to give an extensive manual of the iAdd app.

Part Three: iAdd - The iPhone / iPad App

This is the third part of this ebook, and it's the "down to earth, no blah-blah, real life" part of it. We will not talk about concepts here anymore. We will talk about real things and real actions. We will describe the first iPhone / iPad app which implements the Assess - Decide - Do framework. It's called iAdd and it's available on the AppStore for 3.99 USD (at the time of writing). Just to let you know, iAdd will work on iPhone AND iPad, but more on that in a separate chapter. Bottom line is that you get 3 apps, the iPhone/iPod and the iPad one, for the same price.

iAdd is my first real life implementation of the Assess - Decide - Do framework. I started the app with almost no knowledge of Objective C (I am though a seasoned programmer in PHP) and I finished in 30 days. It was a personal challenge and one of the most demanding coding projects I ever embraced. As a curiosity it's also the first app I ever wrote for the iPhone, in native Objective C.

iAdd aims to keep you balanced and stress free while still managing to get everything your really need to be done, done. It's the most versatile replacement for a traditional ToDo list. It uses standard iPhone user interface elements in order to make your experience as smooth as possible, while still keeping in place all the main characteristics of the framework.

Its interface is the result of countless hours of testing and experimenting. I consider myself a power user when it comes to productivity apps, and as such, I do believe that a productivity app should be as simple as possible. iAdd is not packed with fancy yet disconcerting user interface elements. Because it's not the app that is important, it's you. This is why iAdd will look really simple in the beginning.

iAdd uses Core Data for storage, an advanced storage mechanism created a few years ago by Apple, which makes data traversal and management far more intuitive for a programmer, but also extremely safe for the end user. A Core Data app should easily be ported to any storage backend you may want to, without touching the code. iAdd uses an sqlite backend, which is an industry standard for simplicity and reliability. This data model design allows for a very flexible development for the app in the future. For instance, if need will be, iAdd could be easily be ported into a web based app, accessible from any device.

If you didn't get it so far, you can do it now, before we start diving into it features.

iAdd is available on iTunes as an iPhone/iPad universal app, for only 3.99 USD.

Tap here to buy it now.

What Is iAdd For iPhone/ iPad Good For?

If you suffer from working anxiety, from "not enough done" frustration, from "deadline guilt" or even from "procrastination bulimia", then iAdd is for you. In much simpler words, iAdd will help you to:

add tasks, events and projects from a single insertion point

brainstorm ideas

group tasks in projects, detach them from projects or promote task to projects

move tasks back and forth from ideas and projects

archive tasks, events, projects and ideas into collections, for further reference

assign contexts, start and end dates to your tasks, events and projects focus only on one realm at a time, being it Assess, Decide or Do

enforce the ADD framework on your day to day routine

keep all your data in sync onver the cloud (currently Dropbox is supported)

Overall, iAdd will keep you balanced and stress free. There is one thing that iAdd can't do now, and that is coffee. Hopes are high for the next version, though. ;-)

Framework Compliance

iAdd is 100% compliant with the Assess - Decide - Do framework. Being developed by the creator of the framework (yours truly) helped big time. Seriously, iAdd will enforce the ADD framework on all its major lines, which are:

unique insertion point

complete separation of the 3 realms

specific tasks for each realm: brainstorming only in Assess, time/space projections only in Decide, etc

color code to enforce the approach for each realm (see the introductory chapter for each realm)

iAdd For iPhone Versus iAdd For iPad

iAdd is a universal app. Meaning the same binary will run on iPhone, iPod Touch and iPad without any modifications. In fact, when you buy the app you'll get 3 apps instead of one.

Starting with version 1.2.3, the iPad version is featuring a different interface, in order to take advantage of the iPad bigger real estate. But the iPad version is still 100% compatible with the iPhone in terms of information flow and consistency.

The databases are tied to each device, though. So, keep in mind that you will have a database for the iPad, one for the iPhone and one for the iPod Touch. The good news is that you can keep those databases synced via Dropbox. Don't worry if you don't have an account with Dropbox.com yet, you will be able to create one from within the app.

iAdd will sync your databases over the internet, using Dropbox as a backend. The syncing algorithm will ensure that the latest modification always win. So, if you added a task in the iPhone, then synced it into your iPad, where you modified it, next time you'll sync it to your iPhone you'll get the modified version.

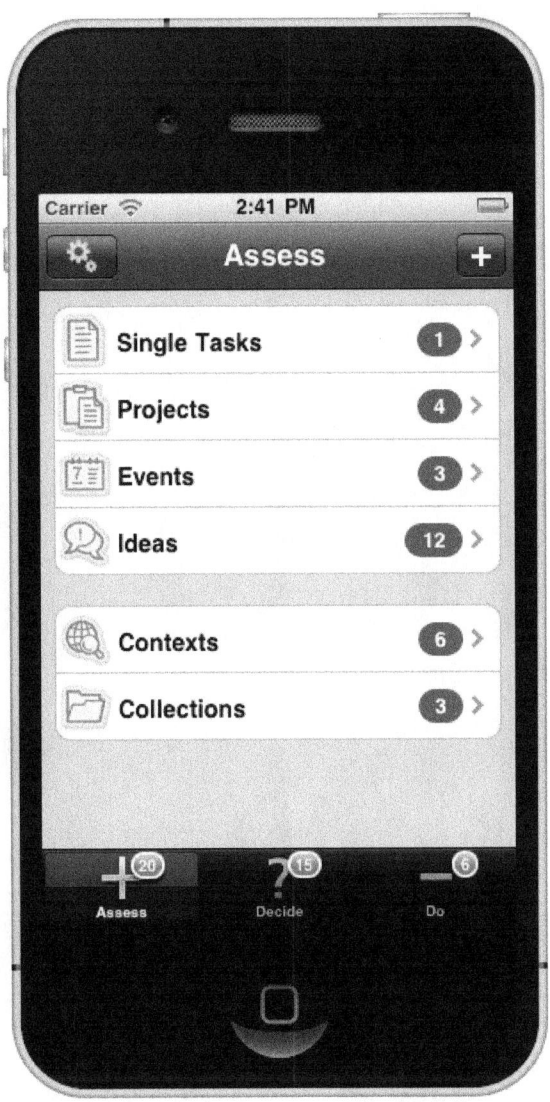

Assess

Realm Definition And Allowed Activities

Assess is the place where you add information. It's the unique insertion point of your system. Here is the place where actually overload the internal processing system with data.

The "Assess" tab bar contains a "+" sign which means that's the only place where you can add stuff. The "Assess" section uses a red-based color scheme. This color scheme is based on a widely recognized international convention for the road signs: when you see red, you gotta stop. This convention is followed on the other two realms too.

As for the allowed activities, in "Assess" you stop and add information. You can brainstorm it, edit it and, once you're happy with the result, you can send it to

Decide, where you will project into a time/space coordinate system (meaning you'll add a context and a start/end date). "Assess" is also the only place where you can delete an item. An item can also disappear from the system once it's done, in the "Do" realm, but deletion happens only in Assess.

Adding Items

In the "Assess" realm, hit the "+" sign on the right top corner. You will be presented with a text field where you can add whatever crosses your mind. Adding items in iAdd follows an inverse pattern: you don't have to choose the specific type of an item and then add it. Instead, you write the information first, and then add the metadata to it. Write something like: "buy milk" because this is on your mind, and then decide if this is a task, an event, a project or an idea.

In much simpler words (and a few images) here's what happens when you add an item:

1. hit the right top "+" button

2. add text in the text field and hit return

3. pick the type of the item: task, event, project, idea

4. see the item in its own view.

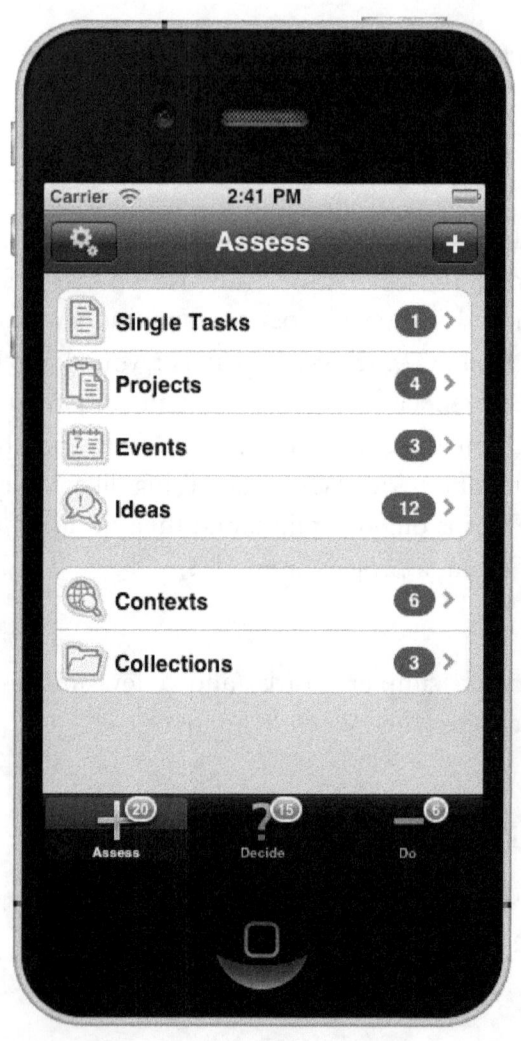

1. In the Assess main view, hit the "+" button

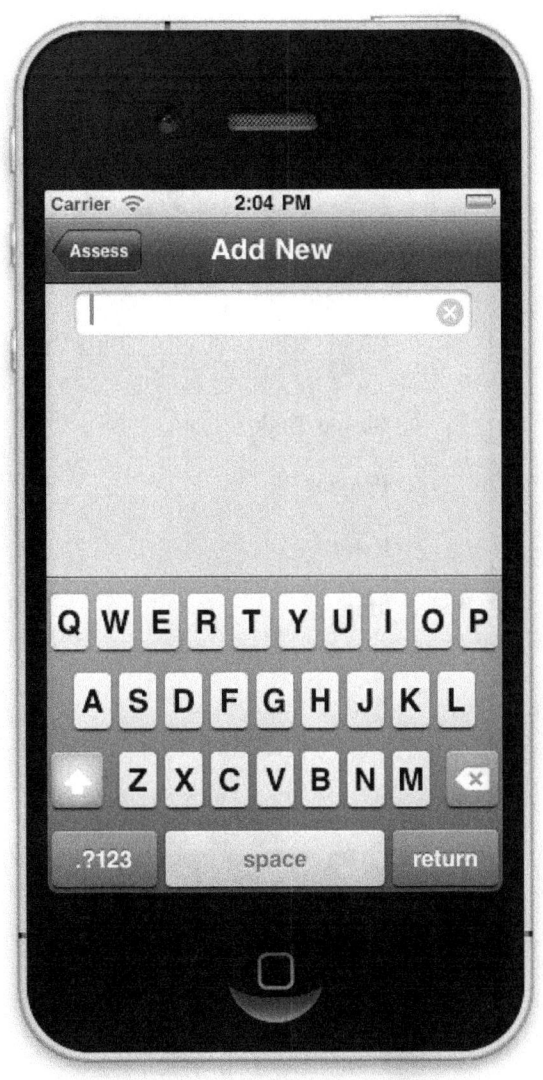

2. Add text in the text field and hit "Return"

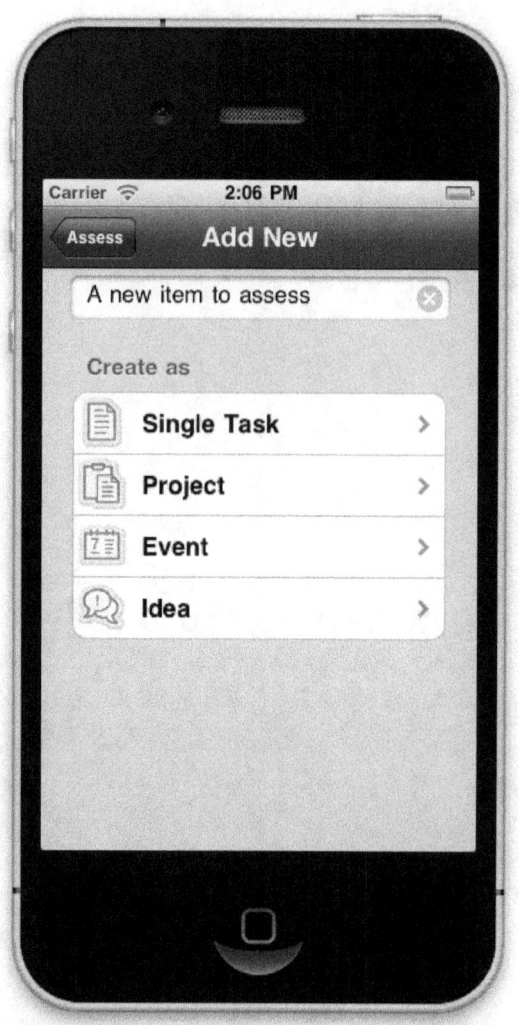

3. Choose item type

4. See the item in its own view

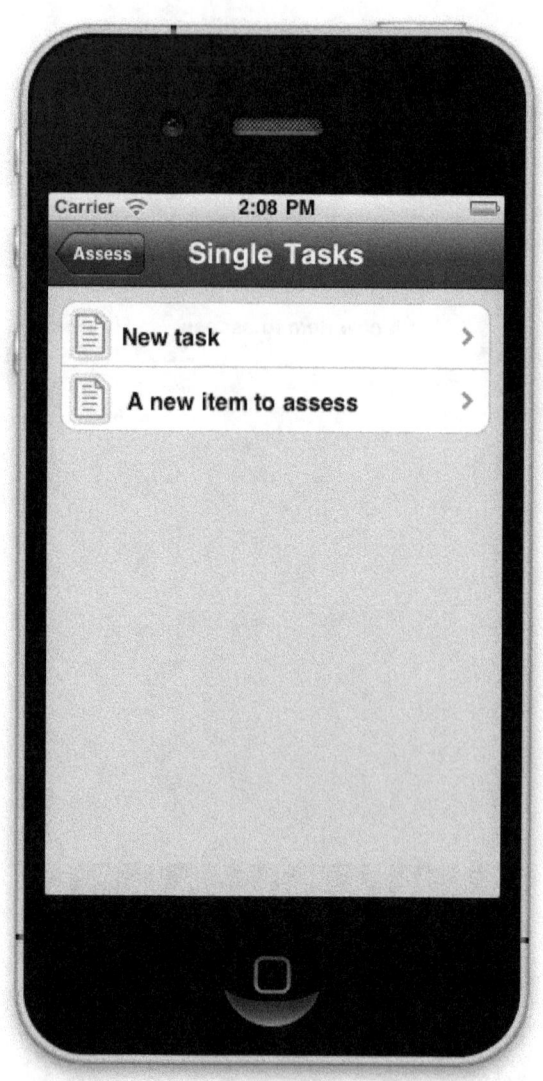

Single Tasks

In iAdd, a Single Task is the smallest actionable entity. It's an independent piece of information, able to carry a context and to be bound by a start and end date. For more complex types of information you can use projects or ideas.

You can access the Single Tasks list from the main "Assess" realm by touching the "Tasks" row. If there aren't any tasks added, touching the row won't have any affect.

Swiping right to left on the list will bring in the standard "Delete" button and you will be able to delete the task from within the list.

Touching a task will push the view containing the task information.

Touching a task in its task view will push the edit view where you can add, edit or delete parts of the task title.

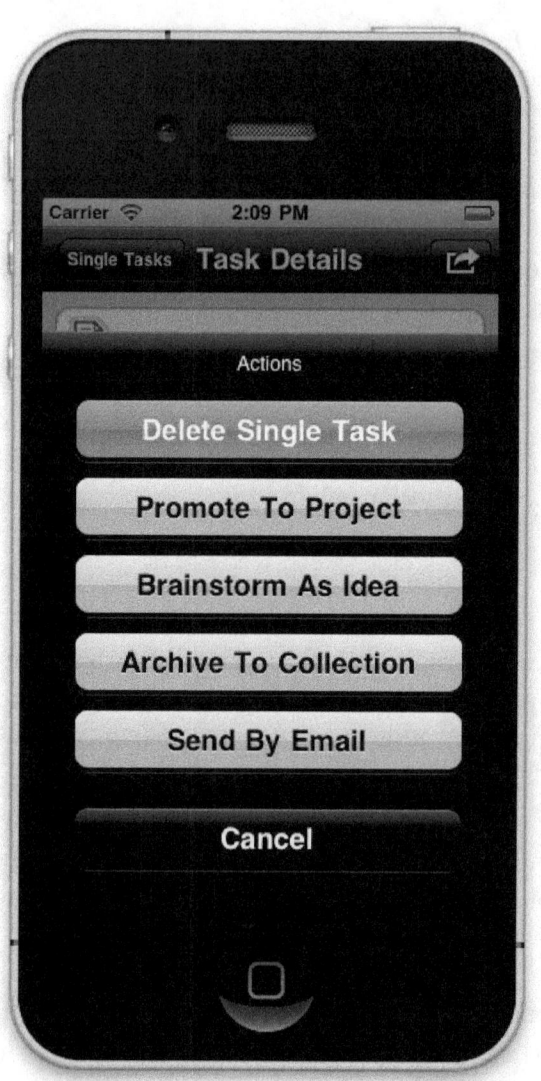

Managing A Task

Touching the top right "Actions" button will bring in an action sheet containing several choices:

Delete Single Task

Will delete the task. It will ask for confirmation first so you won't be able to accidentally delete a task. So no excuses if you do it. :-)

Promote To Project

Will transform the task into a project and take you back to the main "Assess" realm. The newly created project will be accessible in the "Projects" area.

Brainstorm As Idea

Will transform the task into an idea and take you back to the main "Assess" realm. The newly created idea will be accessible into the "Ideas" area.

ARCHIVE TO COLLECTION

Will present you with a choice of collections in which you can store the task for further review. If you don't have any collections created, none will be displayed, of course. Just keep in mind that you will have to create your collection before adding items to it. A collection can hold under the same name tasks, events, ideas and projects. More about collections in their own chapter.

SEND BY EMAIL

Will bring in a modal Mail view for sending the task via email. The subject of the email will be: "New task from iAdd" and the body will contain the task title. After sending the task via email the Mail view will disappear. In order for your email message to be sent you need to have internet access. If not, the message won't be sent and it won't be stored for sending it later.

CANCEL

Will dismiss the action sheet.

Task: Realm-Specific Actions

Once you are satisfied with your task you can send it to "Decide". In that realm you will be able to assign a context, a start and end date and a priority to it. You send a task to the "Decide" realm by touching the orange "Send to Decide" button underneath the task title. Your task will disappear from your tasks list in "Assess" and it will be available from now on under the tasks list in "Decide".

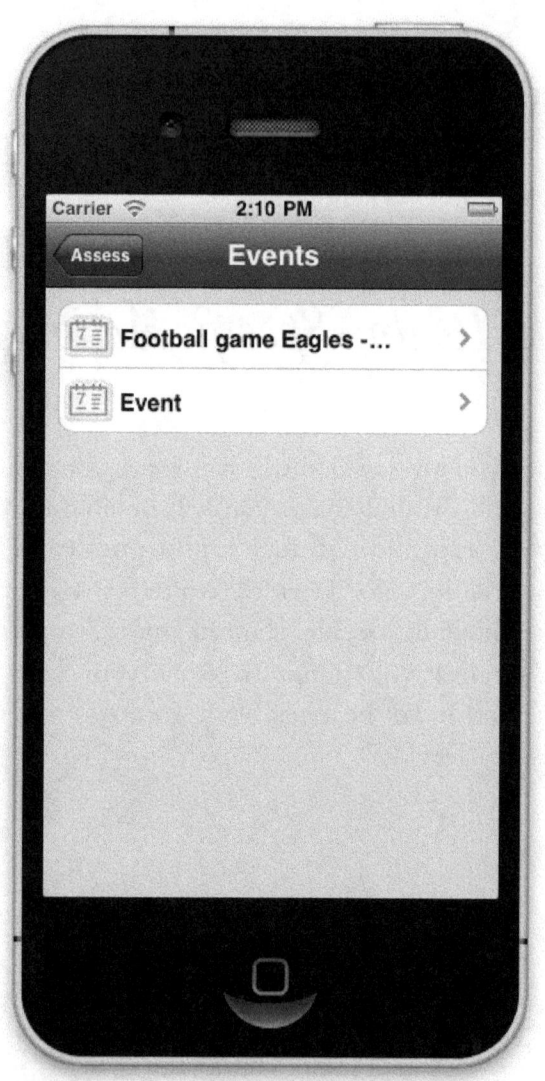

Events

In iAdd, an Event is a type of task which is already bound to a specific location. In other words, you have to be in a specific place in order to do that task. As such, Events have some extra fields compared with a Single Task. More on that in a few paragraphs.

You can access the Events list from the main "Assess" realm by touching the "Events" row. If there aren't any events added, touching the row won't have any effect.

Swiping right to left on the list will bring in the standard "Delete" button and you will be able to delete the event from within the list. Touching an event will push the view containing the event information.

Touching the event title in the event view will push the edit screen where you can add, edit or delete parts of the event title.

Event Data

Events are different from tasks because they carry more metadata in order to be properly defined. An event can't be defined only by its title, like a single task. You need to know its location and start and end dates before making a decision about it. This is why you will add these attributes to an event in the "Assess" stage. The "Decide" realm will only tie the event to a certain context and it will give a certain priority to it.

To add a location and start and end dates to an event, touch the corresponding rows in the event view.

Managing An Event

Touching the top right "Actions" button will bring in an action sheet containing several choices:

DELETE EVENT

Will delete the event. It will ask for confirmation first so you won't be able to accidentally delete an event.

ARCHIVE TO COLLECTION

Will present you with a choice of collections in which you can store the event for further review.

SEND BY EMAIL

Will bring in a modal Mail view for sending the event via email. The subject of the email will be: "New event from iAdd" and the body will contain the event title, the event location and the start and end date. After sending the event via email the Mail view will disappear. In order for your email message to be sent you need to have internet access. If not, the message won't be sent and it won't be stored for sending it later.

CANCEL

Will dismiss the action sheet.

Event: Realm-Specific Actions

Once you are satisfied with your event information you can send it to "Decide". In that realm you will be able to assign a context and a priority to it. You send a task to the "Decide" realm by touching the orange "Send to Decide" button underneath the task title. Your task will disappear from your tasks list in "Assess" and it will be available from now on under the tasks list in "Decide".

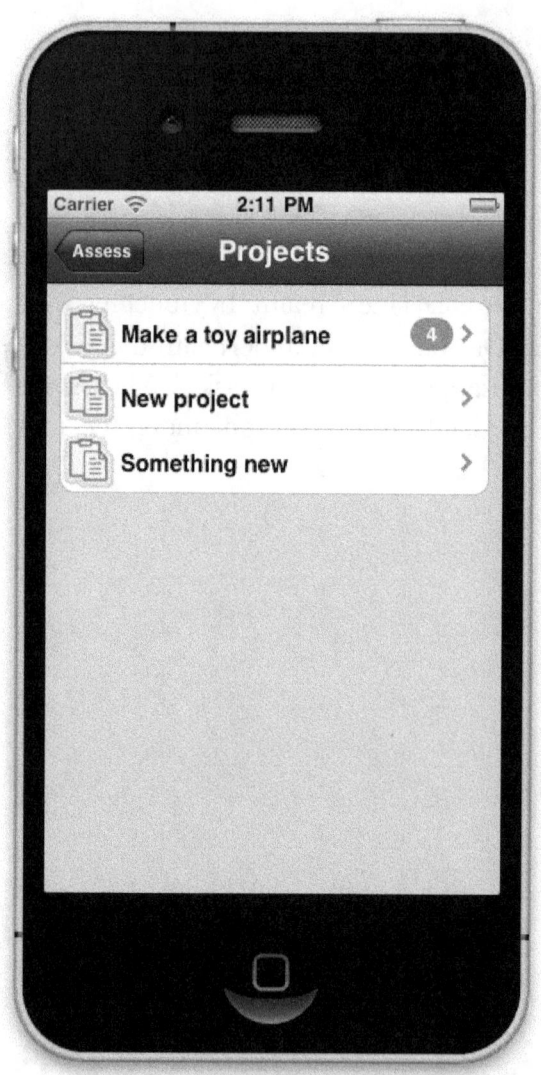

Projects

In iAdd, Projects are unordered collections of tasks. The reason for "unordered" is that the concept of prioritization is not available in the "Assess" realm. In the "Assess" realm you're just brainstorming your goals and put together some pieces of information, without making any decision about them. The prioritization will take place in the "Decide" realm. For this reason, a Project will have a much more "loose" appearance in the "Assess" realm.

You can access the Projects list from the main "Assess" realm by touching the "Projects" row. If there aren't any projects added, touching the row won't have any affect. The Projects list will be different from Single Tasks or Events lists by showing the total number of tasks in each project. If there is no number in the project title row, it means the project has no task yet. An empty project cannot be sent to "Decide".

Swiping right to left on the list will bring in the standard "Delete" button and you will be able to delete the project from within the list. Deleting a project will recursively delete all the contained tasks. Touching a project will push the view containing the project tasks list.

Touching the project title in the project view will push the edit screen where you can add, edit or delete parts of the project title. Touching the first row underneath the project title ("add a task to this project") will push a new view allowing you to add a task for the current project. Tasks will be listed underneath that row in a more or less random order.

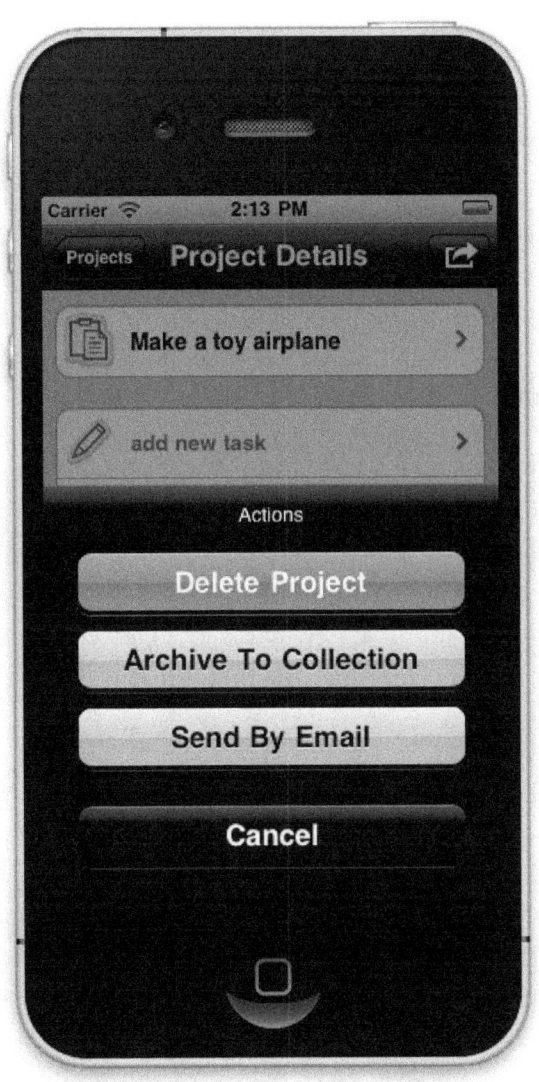

Project Data

The tasks contained in a project are similar to single tasks in structure. But they will be assigned only to that specific project. The tasks within a project cannot be seen in the Single Tasks lists, nor do they count in the total number of items in the "Assess" realm.

A task in a Project can be "detached". If you're navigating to a specific task in a project and touch the top right "Actions" button, the corresponding action sheet will contain a new choice: "Detach Task From Project". If you tap that, the contained task will become a Single Task.

A task in a project can be moved to another project. If you're navigating to a specific task in a project and touch the top right "Actions" button, the corresponding action sheet will contain a new choice: "Move To Another Project". If you tap that, a list of project will appear. By touching a specific project, you will move the task to that project. After that, you will be taken to the tasks list of the initial project.

Managing A Project

Touching the top right "Actions" button will bring in an action sheet containing several choices:

DELETE PROJECT

Will delete the project. It will ask for confirmation first so you won't be able to accidentally delete a project. All the contained tasks will be deleted too.

ARCHIVE TO COLLECTION

Will present you with a choice of collections in which you can store the project, along with all the contained tasks, for further review.

SEND BY EMAIL

Will bring in a modal Mail view for sending the project via email. The subject of the email will be: "New project from iAdd" and the body will contain the project title, and a list of all the contained tasks. After sending the project via email the Mail view will disappear. In order for your email message to be sent you need to have internet access. If not, the message won't be sent and it won't be stored for sending it later.

CANCEL

Will dismiss the action sheet.

d

Project: Realm-Specific Actions

Once you are satisfied with your project description and structure you can send it to "Decide". You send a project to the "Decide" realm by touching the orange "Send to Decide" button underneath the project tasks list. Your project will disappear from your projects list in "Assess" and it will be available from now on under the projects list in "Decide". All the contained tasks will be sent to "Decide" too.

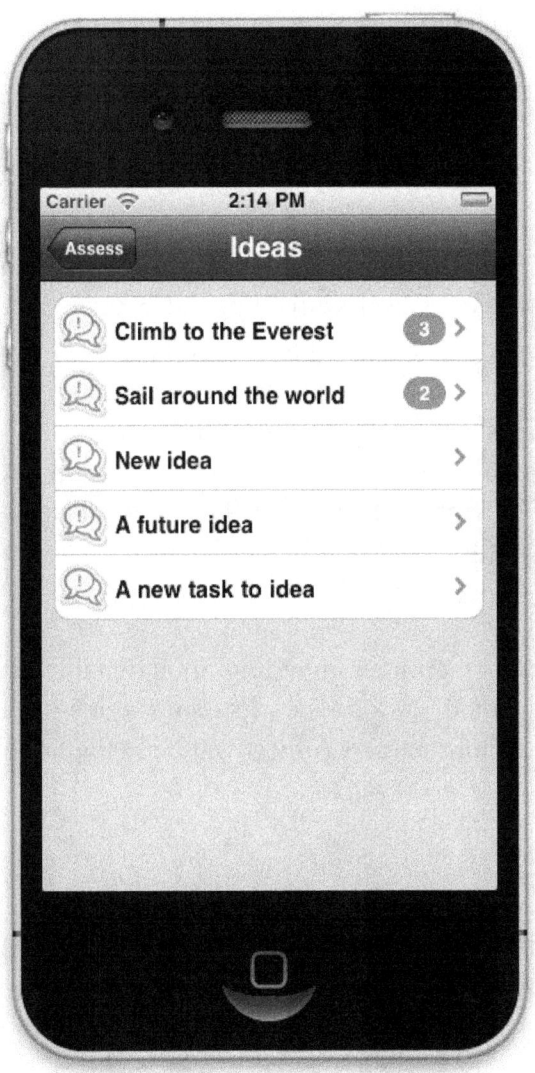

Ideas

In iAdd, Ideas are unordered collections of information. Being very similar to projects, items in an idea are assimilated with "tasks". From a data model point of view, the components of an idea are basically tasks and are interpreted as such. The difference is that an idea is not really an actionable project. It's just a placeholder for brainstorming information. An idea cannot be sent to "Decide". It's a type of data specific to "Assess" only.

But once an idea grew into an actionable list, it can be "promoted" to a project. Its components will become real tasks and the new project will be ready to be sent to "Decide", if need will be.

You can access the Ideas list from the main "Assess" realm by touching the "Ideas" row. If there aren't any ideas added, touching the row won't have any affect. The Ideas list will be identical to the Projects lists, by showing the total number of tasks/details in each idea.

If there is no number in the idea title row, it means the idea has no task/detail yet.

Swiping right to left on the list will bring in the standard "Delete" button and you will be able to delete the idea from within the list. Deleting an idea will recursively delete all the contained tasks. Touching an idea will push the view containing the idea tasks/details list.

Touching the idea title in the idea view will push the edit screen where you can add, edit or delete parts of the idea title. Touching the first row underneath the idea title ("add a task/detail to this idea") will push a new view allowing you to add a new component for the current idea. Tasks will be listed underneath that row in a more or less random order.

Idea Data

The tasks contained in an idea are similar to single tasks in structure. But they will be assigned only to a specific idea. The tasks within an idea cannot be seen in the Single Tasks lists, nor do they count in the total number of items in the "Assess" realm.

A task in an Idea can be "detached". If you're navigating to a specific task in an idea and touch the top right "Actions" button, the corresponding action sheet will contain a new choice: "Detach Task From Idea". If you tap that, the contained task will become a Single Task.

A task in an idea can be moved to another idea. If you're navigating to a specific task in a project and touch the top right "Actions" button, the corresponding action sheet will contain a new choice: "Move To Another Idea". If you tap that, a list of ideas will appear. By touching a specific idea, you will move the task to that idea. After that, you will be taken to the tasks list of the initial idea.

Managing An Idea

Touching the top right "Actions" button will bring in an action sheet containing several choices:

DELETE IDEA

Will delete the idea. It will ask for confirmation first so you won't be able to accidentally delete an idea. All the contained tasks/details will be deleted too.

PROMOTE IT TO PROJECT

Will transform the idea into a project. Every information will remain the same, except from the fact that the idea will be now listed under the "Projects" lists in the "Assess" realm. All the contained tasks will remain unchanged. Also, as a project, the former idea will be now ready to send to "Decide".

ARCHIVE TO COLLECTION

Will present you with a choice of collections in which you can store the idea, along with all the contained tasks, for further review.

SEND BY EMAIL

Will bring in a modal Mail view for sending the idea via email. The subject of the email will be: "New idea from iAdd" and the body will contain the idea title, and a list of all the contained tasks. After sending the idea via email the Mail view will disappear. In order for your email message to be sent you need to have internet access. If not, the message won't be sent and it won't be stored for sending it later.

CANCEL

Will dismiss the action sheet.

Idea: Assess-Specific Actions

An idea doesn't have realm-specific actions. Being just a tool for brainstorming, an idea belongs only to the "Assess" realm.

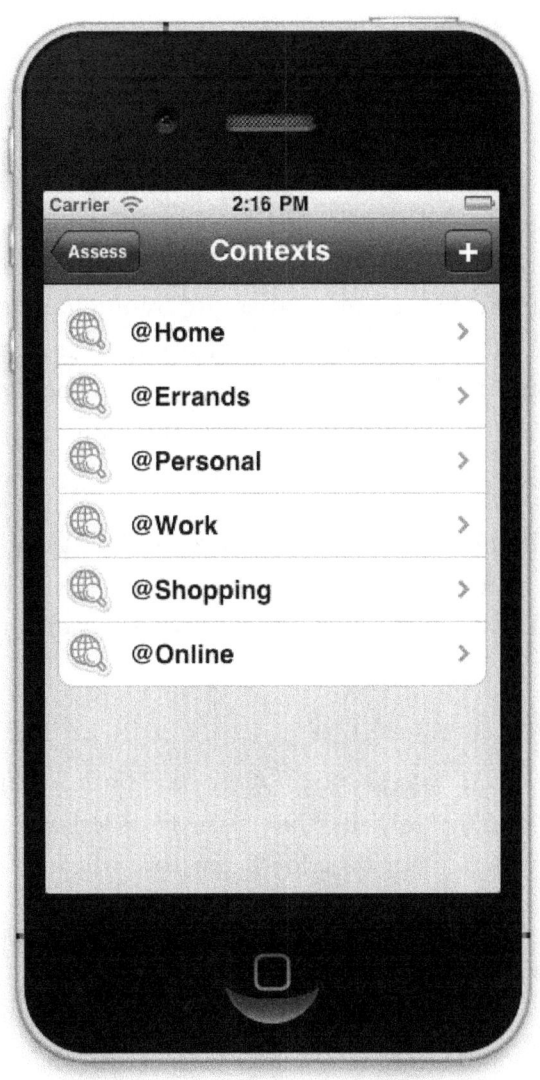

Contexts

In iAdd, Contexts are a way to bind specific tasks to commonly used places. For instance, if a task must be performed around your house, its context would be "@Home". The notation uses the traditional "@" sign in front of the context name. Please keep in mind that you don't need to add the "@" character when you add a context, it will be added by iAdd automatically.

Although you will use Contexts in the "Decide" and "Do" realms, you will add them in the "Assess" realm. The "Assess" realm is the only insertion point in your system.

You can access your Contexts by touching the corresponding row in the "Assess" interface. If you already have contexts added, the row will also display their total number. If there is no context added, touching the row will trigger the adding context view.

You can add more contexts by touching the "+" sign in top right corner.

While in the Contexts list, touching a context will bring in the edit view, allowing you to make modification to its name.

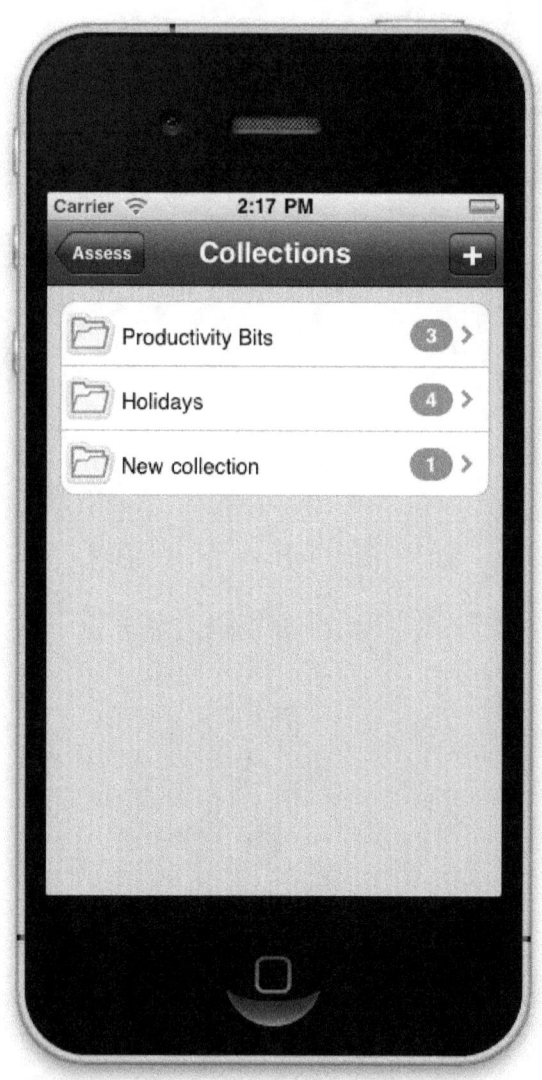

Collections

In iAdd, Collections are a way to organize and store pieces of information for further reference. Each collection can have a different name and can hold Tasks, Events, Ideas or Projects. Usually, you create collections on related topics. You may have some Ideas on a certain field and then some Tasks which you see feasible and also some full-fledged Projects. But you don't have the time or the resources to Decide on that topic right now. Instead of keeping those items in the main Assess interface, you can move them in their own collection, freeing up some work space.

Each item can be eliminated from a collection atomically, at the category level: you can eliminate a task, a project or and idea with all the contained tasks (more on projects and ideas a little later). Taking an item out from the collection is made by touching the button "Re-Assess" from the item detail view, which will make the item available to the Assess realm again.

You can access your Collections by touching the corresponding row in the "Assess" interface. If you already have collections added, the row will also display their total number. If there is no collection added, touching the row will trigger the adding collection view.

You can add more collections by touching the "+" sign in top right corner.

While in the Collection list, touching a collection will bring in list view of the collection, with all the contained items. Touching each item will bring the detail view of that specific item. You can still edit data for all items in a collection, but you won't be able to send them directly to Decide. In order for items to become available for decision, they must be sent to Assess first.

All the other operations you will usually perform with an item (assigning task to a new idea, detaching task from a project / idea, send the task by email) will still be available from within the collection.

While in the collection list view, touching the upper right "Edit" button will let you edit the name of the collection.

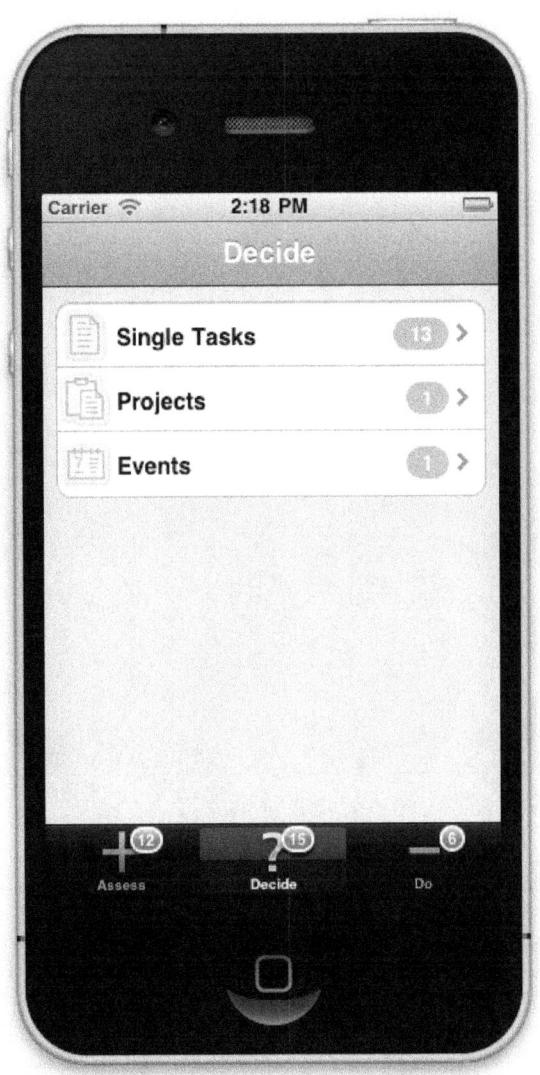

Decide

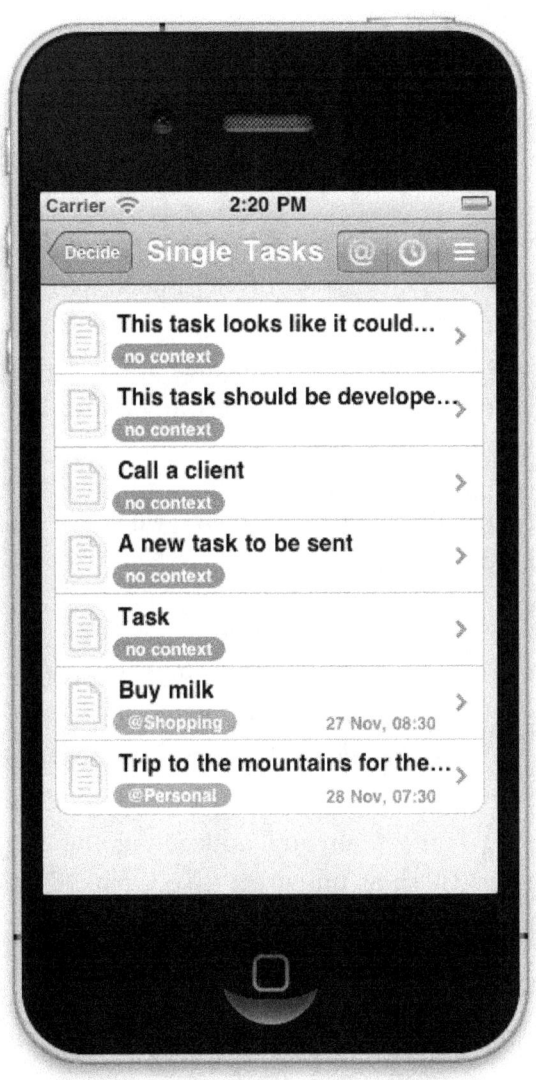

Single Tasks

All the single tasks that have been sent to Decide will appear under the first row of the interface. If there are tasks added, the row will also show you the total number of single tasks available in Decide. If there is no single task in Decide the row won't show any number.

Touching the Single Tasks row will show you a view with all the available tasks.

By default, the list view will show the tasks ungrouped. If you want to group the tasks by context, touch the top right button "@" from the navigation bar. It will be quite usual to have single tasks sent back from Do with a context already added. All the fresh tasks from Assess will show under the "No Context" row.

To revert to the normal list view, touch the top right list button, from the navigation bar, the one near the "@" button.

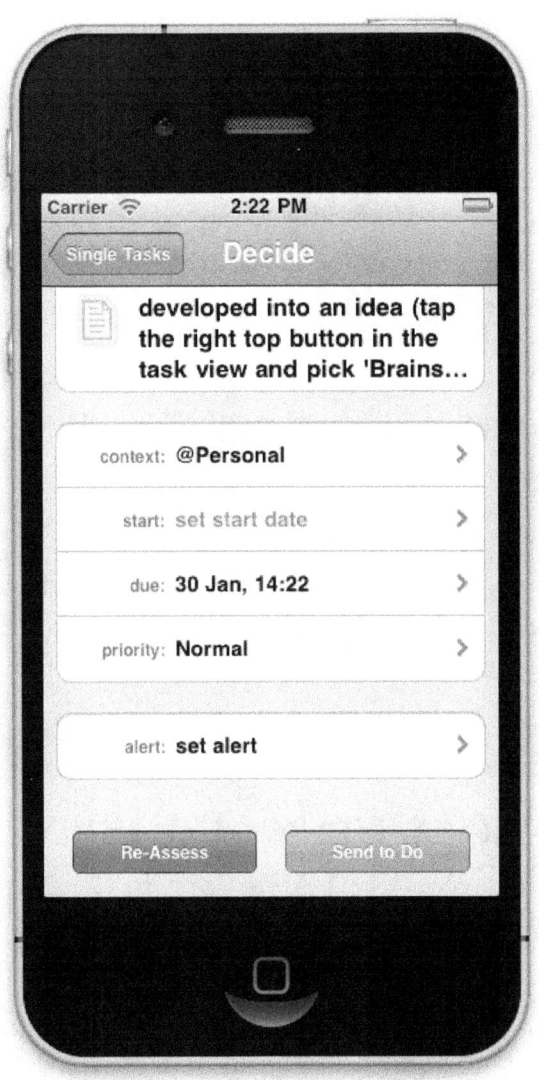

Deciding On A Single Task

While in Decide, you can assign a context, a start and end date, and a priority to a single task. If you are running at least iOS 4.0 you can also set a local alert for a single task.

ADDING A CONTEXT TO A SINGLE TASK

Touch the row "context" and choose a Context from the next view. If there are no contexts added, you will be warned and you should add at least one from the Assess.

ADDING A START AND END DATE TO A SINGLE TASK

Touch the "start" row, or "due" respectively, and pick a date from the date picker. By default, the date picker will show the current date and time.

ADDING A PRIORITY TO A SINGLE TASK

Touch the "priority" row and pick a priority from the next view. Note that at the moment, priorities are just a placeholder for future functionality.

ADDING A LOCAL ALERT TO A SINGLE TASK

Touch the "alert" row and pick an alert interval from the next view. Note that if you are running an iOS version prior to 4.0 the "alert" row won't show up. A local alert will be set and you will be warned at the designated time by a standard system alert.

Single Tasks: Decide-Specific Actions

175

To send a single task back to Assess, touch the Re-Assess button. Please note that if you set attributes to a single task, like context and priority, they will be carried on to Assess. Next time you will send the single task back to Decide from Assess, the old attributes will show up unmodified.

To send a single task to Do, touch the Send To Do button. You cannot send an Single Task to Do if you haven't added a context and at least an end date to it. If you didn't do any of those, an alert will show up and you won't be able to send the task to Do.

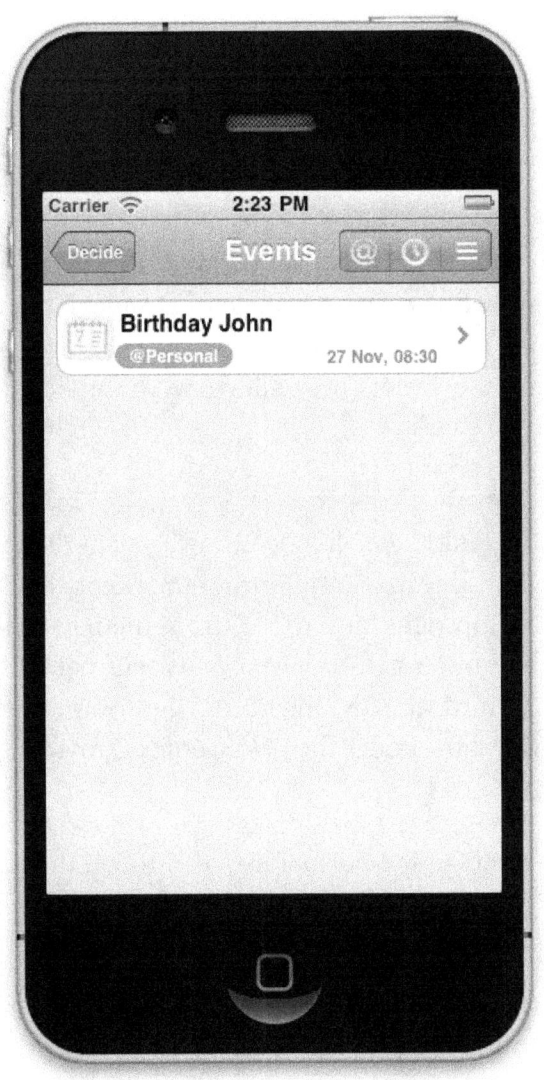

Events

All the Events that have been sent to Decide will appear under the second row of the interface. If there are any events added, the row will also show you the total number of events available in Decide. If there is no event in Decide, the row won't show any number. Touching the Events row will show you a view with all the available tasks.

By default, the list view will show the events ungrouped. If you want to group the events by context, touch the top right button "@" from the navigation bar. It will be quite usual to have events sent back from Do with a context already added. All the fresh events from Assess will show under the "No Context" row.

To revert to the normal list view, touch the top right list button, from the navigation bar, the one near the "@" button.

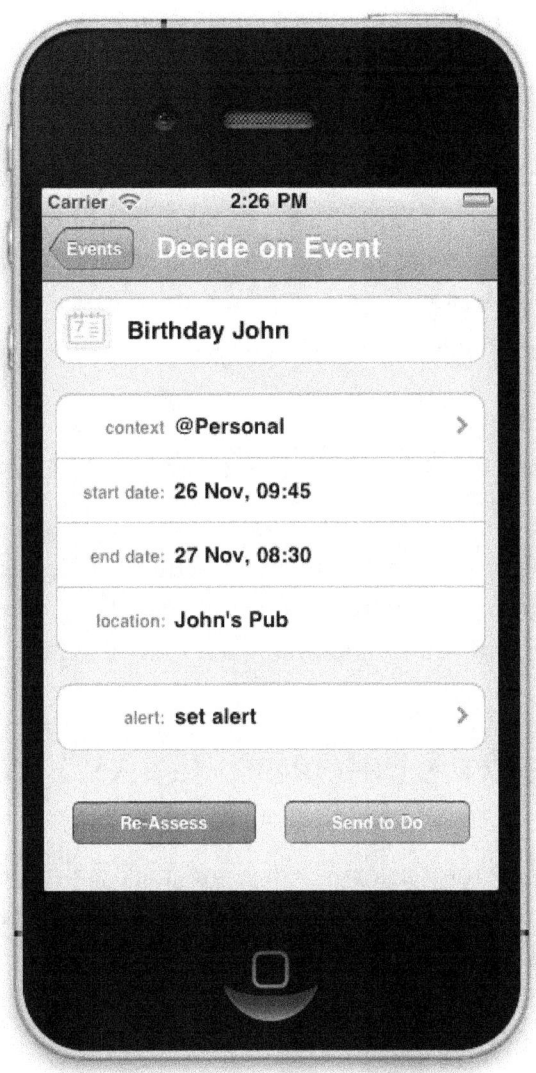

Deciding On An Event

While in Decide, you can assign a context and a priority to an Event. Since you've already set the start and end date of the event, you won't have to do that again in Decide. If you are running at least iOS 4.0 you can also set a local alert for an event.

ADDING A CONTEXT TO AN EVENT

Touch the row "context" and choose a Context from the next view. If there are no contexts added, you will be warned and you should add at least one from the Assess.

ADDING A PRIORITY TO AN EVENT

Touch the "priority" row and pick a priority from the next view. Note that at the moment, priorities are just a placeholder for future functionality.

Adding A Local Alert To An Event

Touch the "alert" row and pick an alert interval from the next view. Note that if you are running an iOS version prior to 4.0 the "alert" row won't show up. A local alert will be set and you will be warned at the designated time by a standard system alert.

Events: Decide-Specific Actions

To send an event back to Assess, touch the Re-Assess button. Please note that if you set attributes to an event, like context and priority, they will be carried on to Assess. Next time you will send the event back to Decide from Assess, the old attributes will show up unmodified.

To send an event to Do, touch the Send To Do button. You cannot send an event to Do if you haven't added a context to it. If you didn't add a context, an alert will show up and you won't be able to send the event to Do.

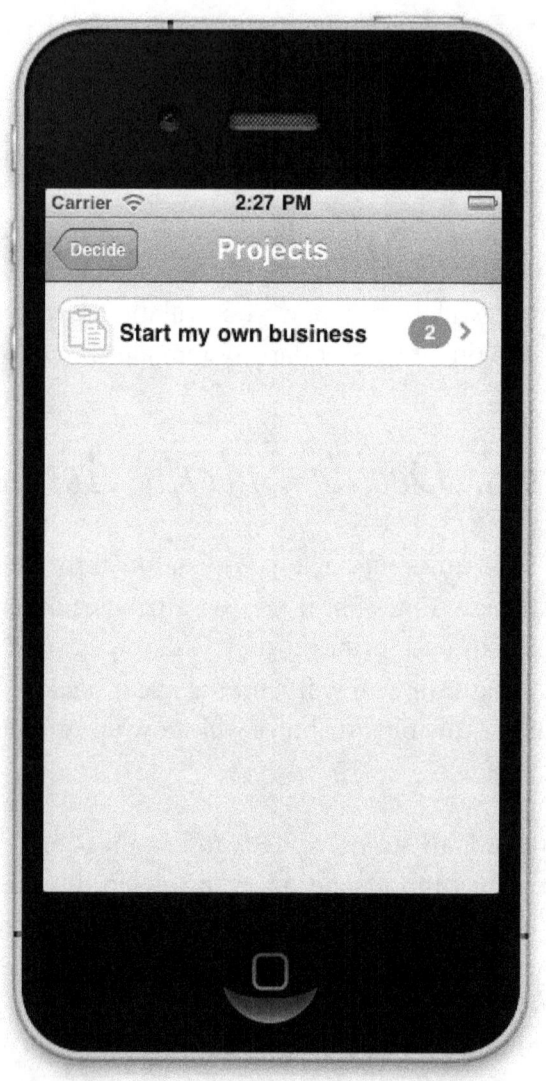

Projects

All the projects that have been sent to Decide will appear under the third row of the interface. If there are projects added, the row will also show you the total number of projects available in Decide. If there is no project added in Decide the row won't show any number.

Touching the projects row will show you a view with all the projects in Decide. If the Projects contains tasks, the row will also show you the total number of tasks in that project.

Choose a project by touching it in the list view. You will be able to see the project title and all the contained tasks listed below. You will also be able to do realm-specific actions at the project level.

To decide on a certain task, touch it from the project detail view. The detail view of a task contained in a project will show up not only the task title but also the title of the contained project. This layout will be carried on in Do too, but more on that on the corresponding chapter.

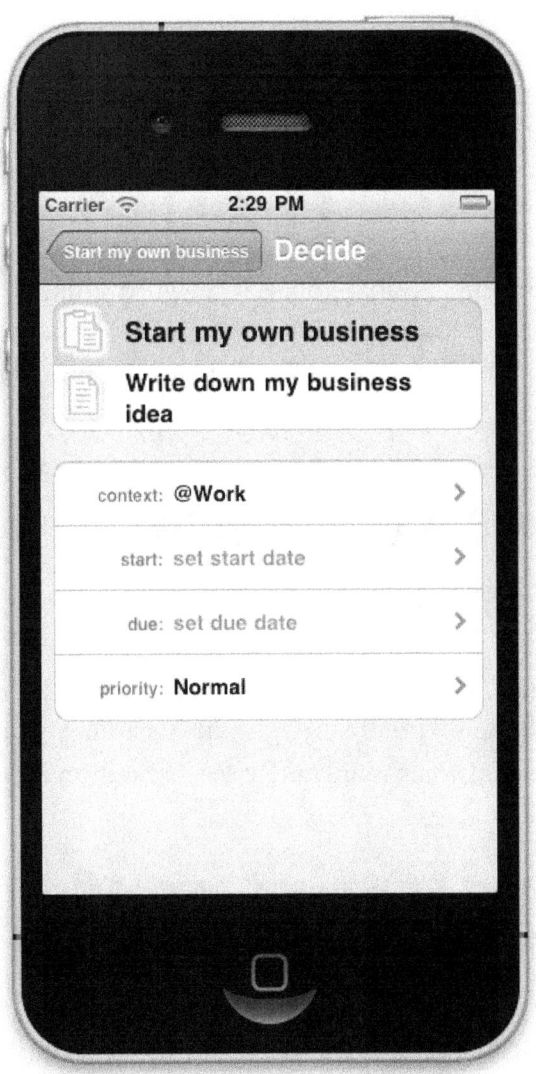

Deciding On A Task From A Project

While in Decide, you can assign a context, a start and end date, and a priority to a task from a project. If you are running at least iOS 4.0 you can also set a local alert.

ADDING A CONTEXT TO A TASK IN A PROJECT

Touch the row "context" and choose a Context from the next view. If there are no contexts added, you will be warned and you should add at least one from the Assess.

ADDING A START AND END DATE TO A TASK IN A PROJECT

Touch the "start date" row, or "end date" respectively, and pick a date from the date picker. By default, the date picker will show the current date and time.

ADDING A PRIORITY TO A TASK IN A PROJECT

Touch the "priority" row and pick a priority from the next view. Note that at the moment, priorities are just a placeholder for future functionality.

ADDING A LOCAL ALERT TO A TASK IN A PROJECT

Touch the "alert" row and pick an alert interval from the next view. Note that if you are running an iOS version prior to 4.0 the "alert" row won't show up. A local alert will be set and you will be warned at the designated time by a standard system alert.

As you add contexts and start and end dates to the tasks contained they will show up in the project detail view. Deciding on a project is a matter of processing al its contained tasks.

187

Projects: Decide-Specific Actions

To send a project back to Assess, touch the Re-Assess button. Please note that if you set attributes to a task contained in a project, like context and priority, they will be carried on to Assess. Next time you will send the project back to Decide from Assess, the old attributes of the contained task will show up unmodified.

To send a project to Do, touch the Send To Do button. You cannot send an project to Do if you haven't added a context and at least an end date to all of its contained tasks. If you didn't do any of those, an alert will show up and you won't be able to send the project to Do until you assign a context and at least an end date to all of its contained tasks.

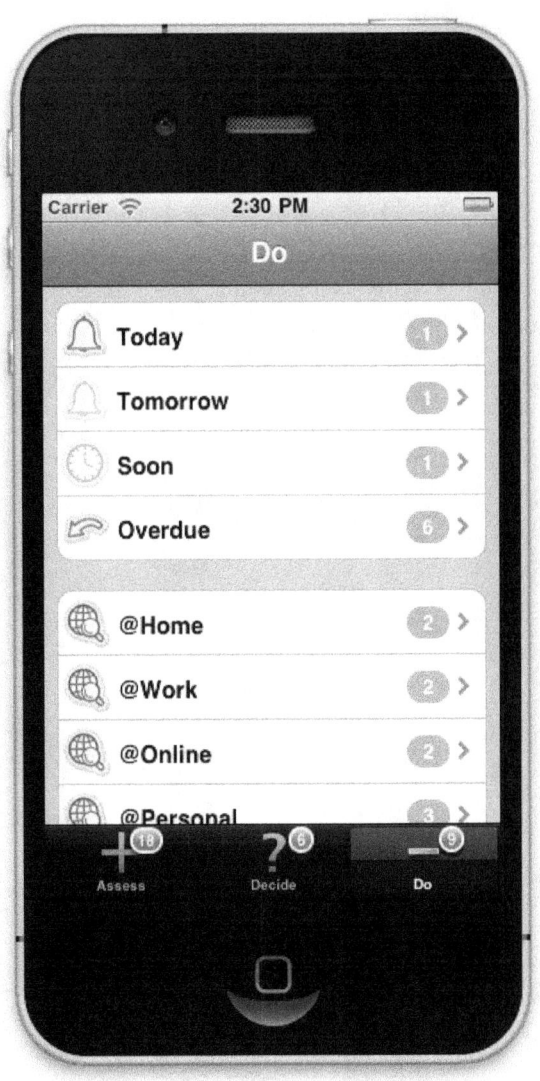

Do

Realm Definition And Allowed Activities

Do is the place where you can see - and cross off - all your pending tasks, events or projects. Do doesn't contain ideas.

The "Do" tab bar contains a "-" sign which means that's the only place where you can take out stuff from your system, by actually doing it, making it happen. The "Do" section uses a green-based color scheme. This color scheme is based on a widely recognized international convention for the road signs: when you see green, you can move on.

As for the allowed activities, in "Do" you can only set a task or event status as "Done" which will delete the item permanently for the database, or you can send it back to Decide. You can also delete projects which doesn't have any contained tasks anymore.

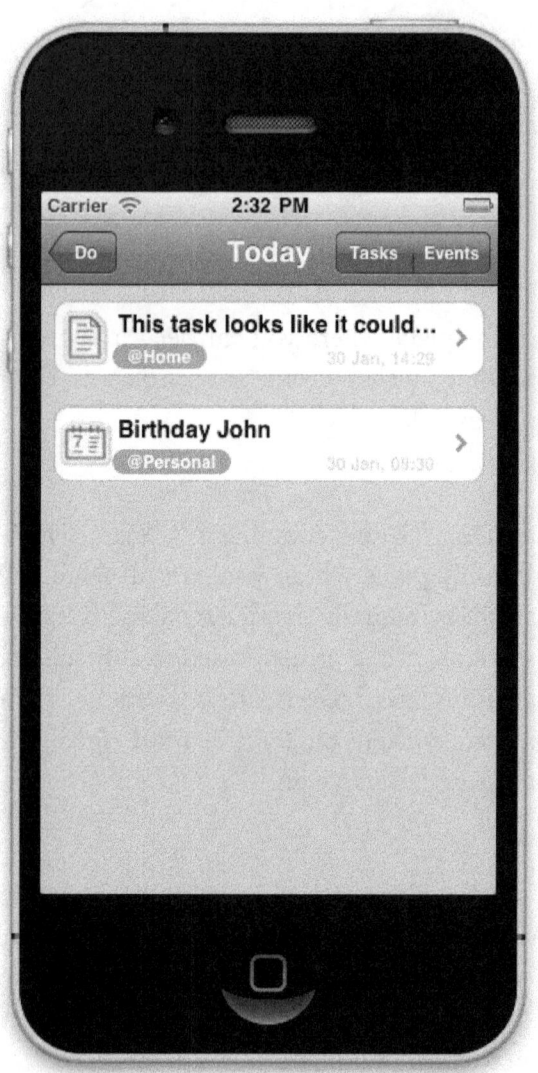

192

Time Based Views

Time based views will show you the tasks and events the way you scheduled in Decide.

If there are any tasks or events available for Today, they will show up under Today. If there are any tasks or events which are not available for today, but they will be available soon, they will show up under Soon. If there are any tasks or events which have the end date before today at 0:00 they will show up under Overdue. Each row will show the total number of tasks and events in that specific time view.

The icons for the time-based views are following the some traffic light color scheme: the Today's icon is green, meaning you can go ahead and do what you have to do, the Soon icon is orange, meaning you have to stay prepared for what's coming, and the Overdue icon is red, meaning you have to stop and re-decide on those tasks (or delete them completely).

If there aren't any tasks or events to fulfill these conditions, the time based views won't show up. Instead, you'll see a placeholder with a nice, uplifting message: "yay, nothing to do today!" It depends on what you understand by "uplifting" but you know what I mean.

In order to see the tasks and events available on each of these time based views, pick one by touching the corresponding row. You will see a list made by 2 sections: tasks and events. The items will appear ordered ascending, the earlier the first.

If you swipe left to right on a row you will bring up the standard "Delete" button, touching it will delete the task or event permanently.

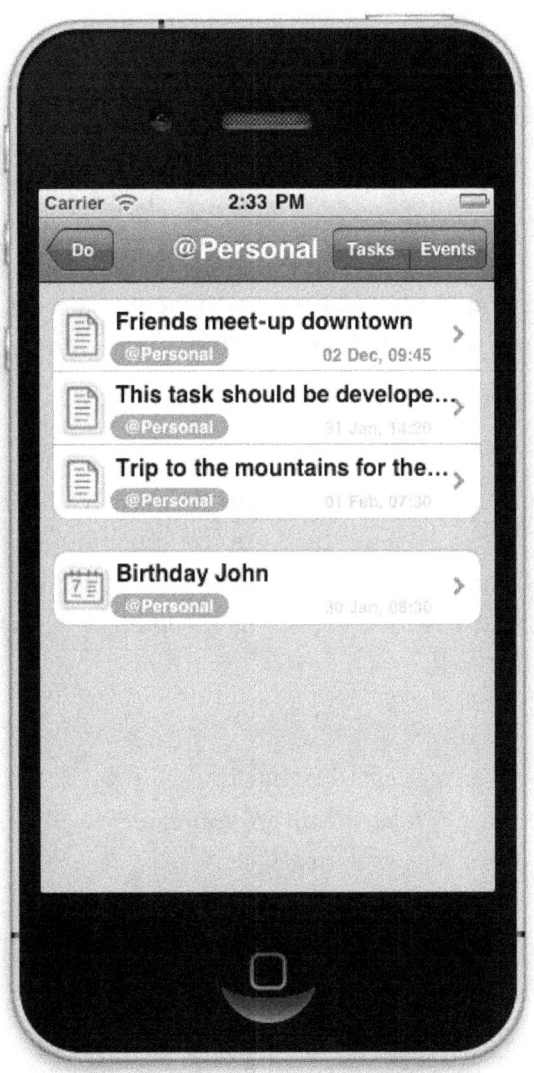

Context Based Views

Context based views will show the tasks and events which have been assigned to a specific context. If there aren't any tasks or events assigned to a context, that context won't appear in the main view of the Do realm. Each row will also show you the total number of tasks and events in that context.

In order to see the tasks and events available on each of the contexts views, pick one by touching it. You will see a list made by 2 sections, exactly as in the time based views. The items will also be ordered ascending, the earlier the first.

If you swipe left to right on a row you will bring up the standard "Delete" button, touching it will delete the task or event permanently.

Switching Between Tasks And Events

The tasks and events lists are sharing a similar behavior, regardless of the specific type, time-based or context-based: you can filter the list view to show only the tasks or only the events in it. In order to see only the tasks or only the events, touch the top-right corresponding button. You will see in the interface only the tasks or the events for that specific time or context based view.

Touching a task or an event will show you a detailed view of that task and event, in which you can see its context, its start and end date and its alert (if you're running an iOS version greater than 4.0). If the task is part of a project, you will also see a row above the task's name, with the name of the project.

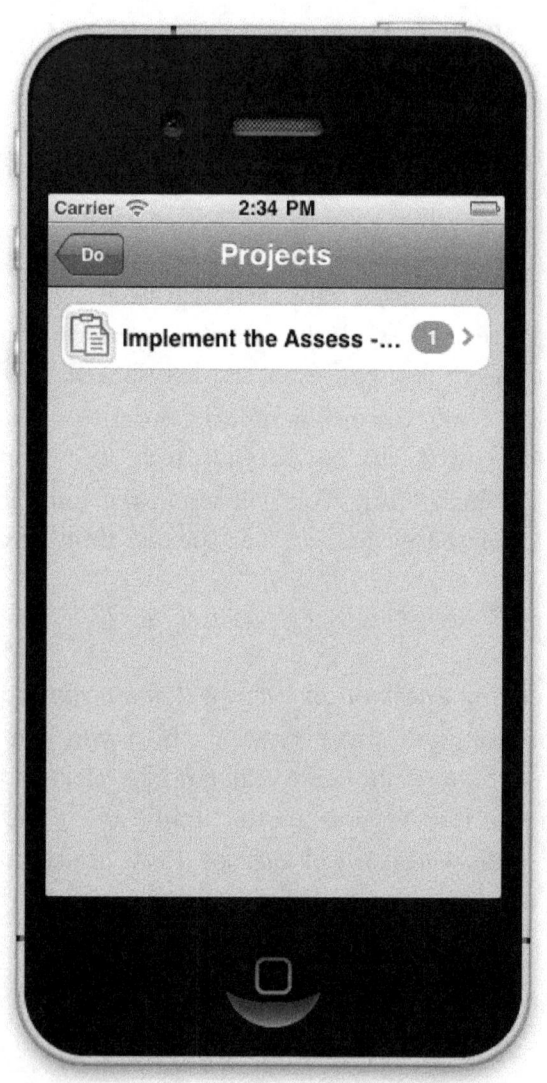

Project Based Views

The third category of views in Do, is the Project views. Although in Do you only have to "do" tasks, the Project based view is provided as a convenient way to follow through the tasks you already organized in a Project. Since all the scheduling is done in Decide, in Do you only have to focus on one task at a time. But having a way of monitoring the projects and their remaining tasks seemed to be a good thing to have in Do.

In the project based view, you can see a list with all the projects which have been added to Do. You can also see a number with the total number of remaining tasks in each project. Touching a project name will bring the project detail view. You will see all the tasks assigned to a project and you will have a chance to process them from within that view. Once a project doesn't contain tasks anymore it will show up in grey in the projects list.

If you want to delete a project from within the project list, swipe left to right and the standard Delete button will appear. Touching it will permanently delete the project and all the contained tasks.

In the project detail view you can choose to re-decide the project or to mark it as done. If you mark it as done, the project and all the contained tasks will be deleted permanently.

Do-Specific Actions

In Do, you can only mark a task, an event or a project as Done, or you can re-send it to Decide.

To mark a task or event as done, touch the "Done" button. The item will be deleted permanently from the database. To send it back to Decide, touch the "Re-Decide" button. Any attributes you set up in Decide will remain unchanged.

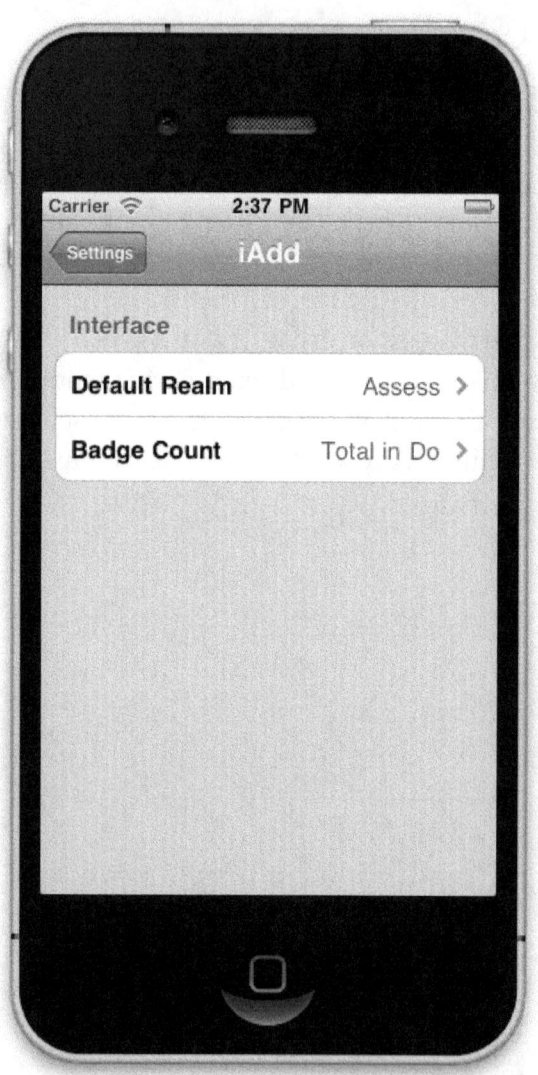

Settings & Syncing

iAdd has two setting so far: one about the default realm in which you want to start the app and the other about the application badge number, or badge count. You can find these settings in the default Settings app for bot iPhone and iPad.

DEFAULT REALM

Go to the iPhone app Settings and scroll down until you find the iAdd icon. Click on that row and choose the setting: Default Realm. By choosing one of those 3 rows, you determine which realm will be shown when you start the app: Assess, Decide or Do.

BADGE COUNT

Go to the iPhone app Settings and scroll down until you find the iAdd icon. Click on that row and choose the setting: Badge Count. You have the following settings available:

None - the app badge won't show any number, regardless of how many items you have in iAdd

Total In Assess - the app badge will show the total number of items in Assess. Please note that Projects and Ideas are counted at the category level, regardless of the number of tasks contained. So a Project or Idea with 7 tasks in it will count as 1 item in Assess.

Total In Decide - the app badge will show the total number of items in Decide. Please note that Projects are counted at the category level, regardless of the number of tasks contained. A Project in decide with 5 tasks will count as 1 item.

Total In Do - the app badge will show the total number of items in Do. That includes all the Tasks, Events and Projects (counted at the category level too)

Total Overdue - the app badge will show the total number of overdue items. The number will include the Tasks and Events which have the end date property before today at 0:00. Please note you have to access the app at least once for the number to refresh (otherwise it will show the number for the last day accessed).

Total Today - the app badge will show the total number of items for Today. The number will include the Tasks and Events which have the end date property before today at 24:00. Please note you have to access the app at least once for the number to refresh (otherwise it will show the number for the last day accessed).

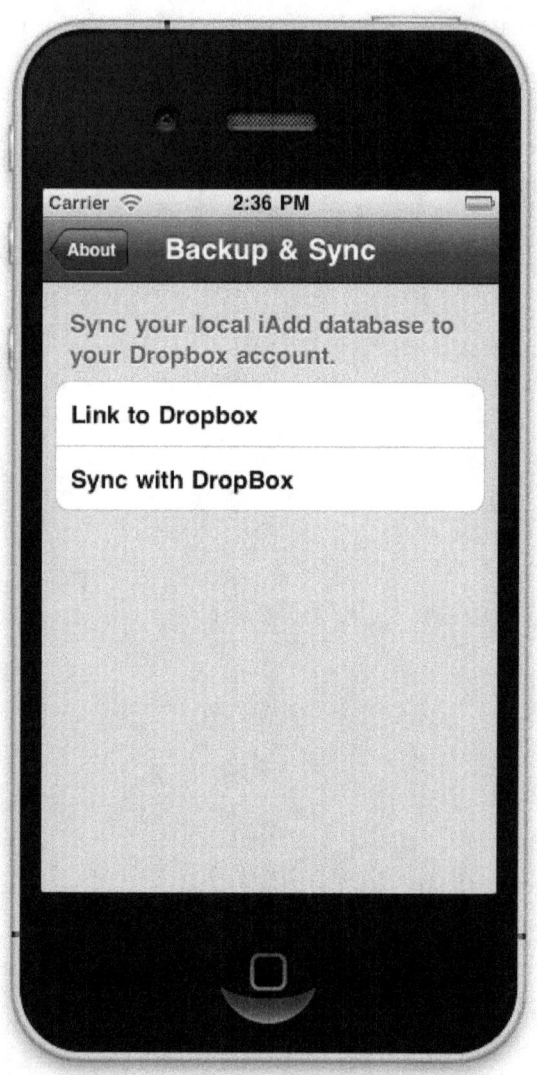

SYNCING

You can sync your iAdd data with Dropbox, one of the most popular cloud storage services on the web. You will need a Dropbox account for that and you can get one for free. Each free account on Dropbox gets 2Gigabytes of storage. For comparison, a regular iAdd backup will take only a few hundreds of kilobytes. If you don't have a Dropbox account you will be able to create one from within the app.

Your iAdd data will be available on a private folder called iAddBackup. It is not advisable to edit manually the files or folders within the iAddBackup folder, otherwise the results of the next sync will be unpredictable.

The backup format for iAdd is JSON. Meaning your data will not be visible as plain text, but instead it will be encapsulated in a special format. JSON is an industry standard in data exchange and it's very robust and practical.

In order to initiate a sync, you should touch the top-left "settings" button in the Assess realm. It will bring a general interface containing information about iAdd, a few help pointers and the Sync part. Touching the Sync & Backup row. You will enter the Sync & Backup view.

Before syncing, you'll have to "link" your iPhone to your Dropbox account. In other words, you will have to login to Dropbox. Touching the "Link to Dropbox" will bring in a form in which you should enter your Dropbox credentials: email and password. If you do not have a Dropbox account, you will be able to create one from this view. In order to do that, touch the "Create an account" link.

After you linked your iPhone / iPad to Dropbox, the row text will change to "Unlink from Dropbox". You may have many Dropbox accounts, but you can link a device to only one account at a given time. So, if you want to use another account for syncing your iAdd data, you should touch "Unlink from Dropbox" and on the next form, enter the credentials for another Dropbox account.

If your iPhone / iPad is linked to Dropbox, all you have to do is to touch the "Sync with Dropbox" row. If there is no Internet connection or if the Dropbox endpoint API cannot be reached, you will be warned. If everything is ok, you should see an activity indicator and the final message should be "Sync completed". Depending on the state of data, the final message can be either "Remote files cleaned up" or "Local files synced". This isn't a sign that the sync didn't complete.

If you want to verify the sync, you can do this by installing the Dropbox free iPhone / iPad app and looking for a folder called "iAddBackup" on your Dropbox folder structure.

iAdd Usage Scenarios

You can use iAdd as a general task, events, ideas and project management tool. Being simple and intuitive, it will allow a good degree of flexibility. What follows are just some simple suggestions on how I am using it and what are some subtle differences between the various types of data iAdd manages.

iAdd for Blogging

I have a lot of blog post ideas while I'm away from the computer. I'm sure you've been there at least once. Before iAdd, I used a mind mapping app on the iPhone to rapidly sketch the idea and send it to me by email. Since I have iAdd, I'm using the Ideas and Projects categories for that. Here's how.

First of all, any blog post starts as an idea. I quickly insert a new Idea and start adding tasks/details to it. Usually it goes up to 8-12 tasks or details. I enter them exactly as I get them in my head. Some of them are simply indications about what I should write about, parts of them are actually sentences I'm going to use in blog post. This first stage ends in about 3-4 minutes.

If I have too many ideas in the Assess interface (too many meaning more than 15) I also take the time to move the freshly added idea into a (previously created) collection called, of course, "Blogging". Now, next time I'm browsing through my collections and feel like working a little bit on my blogging ideas, I start perusing one of the ideas I find there. That means I transform the writing indications into tasks. This process shaves around 30% off of the tasks/details, so I remain with maximum 5-7 tasks in the idea.

At this point, if the idea is in the "Blogging" collection, I hit Re-Assess and move it to the Assess realm. If it's already there, all I do is to promote it to a Project. I then select the Project, send it to Decide and leave it there until I find the time or drive to actually write that blog post. When I know when and how I could write that blog post, I'm moving to decide and assign a context (usually @Blogging) and a time-frame to each task. Most of the time, they have the same end date.

When I'm finished with this (usually in under a minute) I hit "Send to Do" and voila, the blog post idea will appear in my Do realm, under the Projects view. All the contained tasks are grouped and available under the Contexts view (@Blogging, of course) and in the time views. All I have to do now, when I'm into blogging mood, is to switch to my @Blogging context in Do, and implement all the tasks.

The whole process doesn't take longer than 15-20 minutes, including adding idea, its tasks and details, the brainstorming part and all the ADD management (send to Decide, Do, etc).

iAdd For Shopping

This is another earthly usage scenario for iAdd. Everybody goes shopping and does that at least once a week. Shopping lists on the fridge are, in my opinion, not only obsolete, but extremely ineffective. Most of the time, when you realize you need to buy something (other than food) you're NOT near the fridge. So a lot of items will never make it to that list.

Of course there are also tons of other apps designed specifically for that on the AppStore. There's nothing wrong with them. But since you already started to use the framework, it's time to find out how flexible it can be. It could accommodate not only complex projects, brainstorming of ideas but also simple and boring tasks like the weekly shopping.

Here's how I do it. First of all, I create a "@Shopping" context. Then I add into Assess all the items I need to buy. Just the names, without any action. I send them directly to Decide. There, I assign them to the "@Shopping" context I just created. After I finished a batch (usually I add batches of things I need to buy) I group the Single Tasks list view into contexts (the top right "@" button in the navigation bar) and select the "@Shopping" context. All the items I have to do are listed there.

Now, I browse the items and if I know I will go shopping the next day, I add due dates to the items I want to buy and send them to Do. Now, in Do, I will have all the items I need to buy available on the specific date and under the "@Shopping" context. So far, nothing different from what you usually do.

Now comes the tricky part. Every time I buy something from the list in Do, I don't mark it as "Done". I send it back to "Decide". Chances are that I will need to buy that item again some day. If there's food, I will have to buy food again for sure, but it goes also for stuff like cleaning products, printer cartridges or so on. They will stay in Decide for as long as I need them. And they will always be available under the "@Shopping" context in Decide.

In time, I don't have to add almost anything to buy from Assess, everything is already in the system, in Decide. All I have to do is, well, to Decide, when I'm going to buy that stuff. Once bought, the item will go back into Decide, waiting in line for the next shopping session.

Like I told you, I don't like to "kill" a task, it's much better to make it alive again and again.

Single Tasks, Ideas and Projects - Which One To Use When?

As a rule of thumb, a task which cannot be broken down in smaller pieces should be considered a Single Task. That's also the general approach in GTD. But don't sweat on it. I mean, if there's something more general, put it as it comes to your mind and see where it goes. There were a lot of situations when I had to return a Single Task to Decide from Do and from there to Assess, where I promoted it to a Project and started to add sub-tasks to it.

The Assess realm is the place where you can break down your idea into smaller pieces, but as you already know, you cannot predict in advance everything that is going to happen about a task. So, if you find out in Decide, or even in Do, that a Task is way bigger than an atomic part of information, send it back to Assess and start growing it.

This pattern will ensure a natural flourishing of your activity. It will help you think in flows, rather than in deadlines or fixed duration projects. There's nothing wrong with fixed duration projects, of course, but when you realize you can do so much more, there's no reason why you wouldn't do it. ADD will actually enforce a way of growing your ideas and incorporating them into your current projects, rather than stop you in the middle of them.

Single Tasks And Tasks In Projects/Ideas

One of the most subtle differences between Single Tasks and tasks contained in an Idea/Project is about its freedom to move around. If you pay close attention to the available actions for a Single Task and for a task contained in an Idea or Project, you will notice some differences. In short, here's what happens:

A Single Task can only be "promoted" to a Project or an Idea. It cannot be assigned to a Project or an Idea.

A task already in a Project or an Idea can be freely moved in and out of the parent. It can be detached, becoming a Single Task, or it can be assigned to another Project or Idea.

The reason for this behavior is that, in my experience, we tend to group the most important part of information in the first few words. Basically, when we start thinking at a task, we think at the most important part of it. Hence, the Single Task existence. But the next logical step is to grow that piece of information into the next available structure: a Project or an Idea (which can contain other tasks). At this point, we can continue to add the rest of our information to the new structure.

We do not think in a linear way, that's true, but we do write it down linearly. We take it out of our head in a linear, consecutive manner. This is why I don't encourage the "assignment" of Single Tasks to Projects. It's not a natural approach. A Single Task will have to grow organically into a Project or an Idea. A task contained into a Project can also become a Single Task, by detaching it. So, if you want to grow a project, add a new task to it. If you want to move tasks from a Project to another one, do it. They're already IN a Project.

It seems a little bit counterintuitive at the beginning, but you'll soon realize that this is our brain expected behavior. We think in Single Tasks, then we grow those Single Tasks in Projects or Ideas. So, don't break this flow by trying to "assign" a Single Task to a Project, it will only create confusion. iAdd won't let you do that, anyway.

Events vs Tasks

An event is a task which already have its place defined. This is why you add the location of the event in Assess. It's a part of it and you cannot take it out from it. In this case, the context is much more general than the location. Another difference between tasks and Events is the event fixed duration. A task may or may not have a start date (and you will see that in Decide, when you can easily skip adding a start date to a task) but an event is defined by the start and end dates. Again, this is why you add the time components to an Event in the Assess realm.

In my own experience, I didn't have to deal with events as often as I had to deal with tasks. But keep in mind that my social life is rather scarce at this moment (for various personal reasons). But that doesn't mean it won't be as rich as it used to be 2 years ago, before I sold my company. I remember that at that time I had to deal with at least 4-5 events daily, from business meetings to brainstorming , social events and so on.

So, I do think Events have to be incorporated with their own specificity into the app, as long as you understand the differences: an event has always a physical location associated to it and a fixed duration, and both are a part of the event structure, hence you have to take care of them in the Assess Realm.

Where To From Here?

That's it. You made it till the end. I hope you enjoyed reading this ebook as much I enjoyed writing it. I also hope you realized that what you've just read is not a rigid, inflexible system that you have to follow blindly. It's a wireframe, a blueprint, a framework. A life management framework.

It's a foundation you can use to create your own system. It's a scaffold for the house of your dreams. All you have to do now is to start building on it.

Good luck!